CHARACTER OS FOR PROFESSIONALS

Reboot Yourself for Peak Performance

BENJAMÍN ALICEA-LUGO, PHD

Copyright © 2025
BENJAMÍN ALICEA-LUGO, PhD
CHARACTER OS FOR PROFESSIONALS
Reboot Yourself for Peak Performance
All rights reserved.

No part of this publication may be reproduced, distributed, or transmitted in any form or by any means, including photocopying, recording, or other electronic or mechanical methods, without the prior written permission of the author, except in the case of brief quotations embodied in critical reviews and specific other non-commercial uses permitted by copyright law.

BENJAMÍN ALICEA-LUGO, PhD

Printed Worldwide
First Printing 2025
First Edition 2025

10 9 8 7 6 5 4 3 2 1

Interior Book Design by Walt's Book Design
www.waltsbookdesign.com

Discover more at: CharacterOSReboot.com
info@CharacterOSReboot.com

CHARACTER OS
FOR PROFESSIONALS

TABLE OF CONTENTS

FOREWORD 1
   Dr. Vincent Sasso, Principal of Old Bridge High School, NJ
INTRODUCTION 3
   Time for Your Character Reboot
CHAPTER 1 13
   Character: Is it Your Greatest Professional Asset?
CHAPTER 2 25
   How to Unlock Your Character Database?
CHAPTER 3 39
   Maximizing Your Internal Code
CHAPTER 4 55
   From Autopilot to Intention: Discovering Your New Operating System
CHAPTER 5 69
   The Four Pillars of Character: Your Developmental Blueprint
   Character Chart 86
CHAPTER 6 87
   The "Being" Pillar: Clean, Life-Sustaining Water
   TABLE A 88
CHAPTER 7 105
   The "Feeling" Pillar: Vital and Invisible Oxygen
   TABLE B 106
CHAPTER 8 119
   The "Doing" Pillar: A Real and Meaningful Environment
   TABLE C 120
CHAPTER 9 135
   The "Becoming" Pillar: Dynamic & Forward-Moving Energy
   TABLE D 136
CHAPTER 10 151
   Your Character OS Tune-Up Manual: Live the Life!
CHAPTER 11 165
   Your Game is the Long Game
   In Conclusion: Create Your Own Masterpiece 172
APPENDIX 1 173
   Roots of Character OS: Historical Perspectives and Ancient Wisdom
APPENDIX 2 193
   Modern Character OS Development: From Science to Practical Application

FOREWORD

Dr. Vincent Sasso, Principal of Old Bridge High School, NJ

As the leader of Old Bridge High School in New Jersey, I am continually reminded of the pivotal role character plays in both education and life. With a campus community of more than 3,000 students and staff, my work has centered on leading with purpose and fostering unity around a shared vision of academic, social, and emotional growth. Building trusting relationships, leading transparently, and anchoring every strategic decision in the best interests of students have been my key priorities throughout my career.

At Old Bridge High School, character education is not an initiative; it is a cornerstone of who we are. Since 2014, we have proudly been recognized as a National School of Character because we understand that academic success, while vital, is incomplete without ethical reasoning, empathy, and personal responsibility.

This book provides a thoughtful framework for translating those values into meaningful action. I particularly appreciate the way it showcases the narratives of everyday heroes, such as teachers, parents, and students, who demonstrate that character is not innate but instead developed through intentional effort. Its central message is clear: character is essential to educational success. In my experience, students who demonstrate perseverance, integrity, and sound judgment consistently excel. Research from the Character Education Partnership affirms this, showing that character-focused programs lead to stronger school climates, fewer behavioral issues, and higher achievement. The author weaves this evidence together with practical strategies—such as journaling, service opportunities, and community projects—that educators and parents alike can use to help young people grow.

What distinguishes this work is its focus on actionable growth. Rather than resting in theory, it offers daily practices to build honesty, resilience, and emotional intelligence. These recommendations closely align with our district's social-emotional learning efforts, which aim to enhance both student well-being and academic performance.

As we celebrate unprecedented access to information and technology, we also face challenges that test our shared values. In this environment, cultivating character is no longer optional; it is essential. This book arrives as a timely resource for parents raising children of integrity, for educators committed to holistic development, and for leaders building organizations on ethical foundations.

Throughout my journey from classroom teacher to administrator, I have learned that technical skills alone never define effective leadership. The leaders who inspire others and create lasting impact are those who do the hard work of developing moral courage—the courage to live by our school motto and "Do the Right Thing." I often reflect on the quiet moments that reveal our character: a student returning a lost wallet, a teacher acknowledging and correcting a mistake, a leader listening longer than is convenient. These acts rarely make headlines, but they shape culture, build trust, and remind us of who we aspire to be.

This book is a trusted companion in that work. I wholeheartedly endorse it for anyone seeking personal growth or striving to help others grow. Its message is simple and profound: character is not a destination but a lifelong journey—and one worth pursuing.

Vincent Sasso, EdD

Old Bridge Public Schools, New Jersey

INTRODUCTION

TIME FOR YOUR CHARACTER REBOOT

Tony Robbins

"It is not what we get. But who we become, what we contribute...that gives meaning to our lives."

Reasons Your Career Might Be at a Standstill

You are reading this book because something doesn't feel right. You're driven, you've got talent, you've achieved a lot, and you've dedicated years, maybe even decades, to your profession. Yet, somehow, you've hit an invisible wall. The steady climb you were on has leveled out into a frustrating plateau. You see others getting promotions, exciting projects, and recognition. Meanwhile, your career seems to have stalled. You feel stuck, overlooked, and really frustrated. You find yourself working harder than ever, but your efforts just aren't compounding into the progress you expect and deserve. It's a quiet, nagging feeling that the old rules no longer apply to you.

Your career, which had been moving forward, suddenly comes to a standstill. This can leave you feeling stuck and unfulfilled, even with your impressive skills, extensive experience, and intense dedication. You have worked hard on your resume. It shows your skills, knowledge, and innovative strategies. But promotions keep passing you by. You feel less visible at work, and your career seems to stall. This can be confusing and discouraging. It is akin to using outdated software in a rapidly evolving world. You need to update your internal system, which is your Character OS, to break through that invisible barrier and move ahead.

We have all had those annoying moments when our computer freezes. The loading wheel keeps spinning, and our frustration grows. Everything comes to a sudden halt. Think about your job. You are a motivated person, but now you feel stuck. You see your potential, but your coworkers are moving forward without you. The methods that used to work well now seem ineffective. Ideas vanish without any trace. Meetings end without making a real difference. Professional relationships feel more like transactions than genuine connections. This intensifies the sense of immobility. This challenge is not just about getting more skills or tools. It is about your Character OS. This is your mindset and emotional framework. It affects how you handle stress, build relationships, and lead during tough times. It needs a complete reboot to work efficiently.

Trying to fix a computer that keeps crashing by just adding more apps or upgrading hardware doesn't work if you don't fix the central system. Similarly, you can't revive a struggling career without addressing the fundamental issues first. Many professionals spend time and money on certifications. They attend workshops and learn about new technologies. They often overlook the quiet force behind everything: their character content. Resilience, integrity, courage, humility, and accountability are the foundation of authentic leadership. Your technical skills function like specialized applications. Your Character OS, however, is the leading platform that runs everything. It shapes how you respond to challenges and how you build trust with others. Trying to work with an old internal system today is like playing a new video game on a computer from 2005. It just does not work well. You get crashes and delays, and you miss out on opportunities.

Let us examine how a person's character influences outcomes in high-pressure situations. In organizational psychology, emotional intelligence often beats technical skills in leadership roles. Research shows that self-awareness and empathy are key to success in leadership. Daniel Goleman's work on emotional intelligence emphasizes this (see Chapter 7). However, many people overlook these traits until they face a career crisis that prompts them to pause and reflect on their lives.

A Story of Two Character Operating Systems

Meet David, a senior director with an excellent track record of achievements, who has clear and innovative plans. He emerged as a strong candidate for the vice presidential role. Everyone, including David, expected him to move up. He was overlooked. The feedback mentioned vague issues, such as needing "more robust connections" and "enhanced leadership presence." This left him shocked because his skills were impeccable. He did not realize the issue was not his skills. The real problem was with his Character OS. When he encountered an unexpected challenge in the project, he began to micromanage the situation. He emailed his team every hour. He questioned their choices and requested detailed updates. This created anxiety instead of encouraging new ideas. When feedback arrived, he became defensive. He pushed back against it. These were classic outputs of an EgoOS system, which runs threat-assessment scripts in the face of perceived failure. This changed growth discussions into conflicts. This action destroyed relationships rather than fostering them. These were not choices he had made intentionally; they were automated patterns from his outdated internal software. They weakened his otherwise perfect set of skills for work.

Now, contrast this with Maria: Another contender had impressive technical skills. Her dynamic and adaptive nature made her stand out to decision-makers. When a similar challenge arose in her project, Maria remained calm. She didn't point fingers. Instead, she brought her team together with a simple statement: "This is challenging. What do we know?

What do we need? Let's solve this together." Her approach brought calmness and made her team feel valued and important. This led to new ideas that improved the original plan. She became more than just a manager. She became an inspirational leader who spearheaded a movement. Upper management saw her presence, trust, emotional control, and resilience. These qualities were not merely abstract concepts or technical applications. They were actions she showed when things got tough. This suggests that promotions at this level are more dependent on character than on resumes.

Why Character Matters More as You Climb Higher

As you progress in your career, your character becomes increasingly evident. This includes your integrity, values, and behavior. Others, including peers, bosses, and team members, will closely watch you. At the start of your career, technical skills help you move ahead. You complete tasks, follow protocols, and deliver results, and that's enough. As you transition into leadership, your success increasingly relies on who you are. It's about managing stress and handling diverse opinions effectively. It's about taking responsibility and handling uncertainty smoothly. Little habits can cause significant issues. Avoiding tough talks, always needing to be right, or ignoring constructive feedback can create blind spots. These issues can harm your reputation, disrupt team dynamics, and hinder your career advancement. Experienced professionals often feel confident. This confidence might make us too comfortable. It might lead you to believe that past successes will continue to occur without any changes. This concept is known as the "success trap" in leadership psychology. It warns us not to depend too much on old habits. The world changes rapidly, and we must continue to evolve to remain relevant. Sticking to old habits in a changing world is like using the same password for years. It may seem straightforward and convenient, but it can be hazardous. This approach might hurt your ability to lead and put your career at risk.

The Good News: Character is Programmable

Here's the exciting part—you're not stuck with the character you have right now. Who you are today is not the limit of who you can be. Your character is adaptable, vibrant, and ready to grow. This situation is similar to updating your phone or computer. You don't just toss it out; instead, you upgrade it. This makes it work faster, smarter, and more securely. A "Character Reboot" functions similarly. It's about being honest with yourself. Consider how you feel and behave. Identify any obstacles you may be facing. Let go of the old habits that no longer serve you. Swap them out for new ones that align with your values and aspirations. This is not about changing who you are; it is about becoming the best version of yourself.

Upgrading your character makes a noticeable difference in every aspect of the game. You'll handle stress with calm confidence, express your ideas clearly, and foster trust rather than conflict in your relationships. You'll make decisions faster and wiser because you'll know precisely what matters to you. Over time, these changes won't just make you feel better—they'll create real, lasting results. Your relationships will grow stronger, and your leadership will sharpen. Your life will run smoothly because you'll be operating from your strongest, most authentic self. The tools to transform your character are already in your hands—you have to choose to use them.

You Are in Control of Your Reboot

As the book title states, "Reboot Yourself." This framework is a personalized way for you, an ambitious professional who feels stuck, to refresh your character traits and redefine what success means for you. You show what success means in your job and values. You set rules to improve your Character OS and take steps to build your own path. You show what success looks like in your career and values. You set parameters for improving your Character OS. You create a unique path by matching your daily actions with your natural strengths. By examining yourself closely, you can gain a deeper understanding of who you are. You can identify old habits or thoughts that are holding you back. You can also face challenges and clear your mind. This all comes from your understanding, not from what others think. You will look at your progress. You'll see how new habits and responses work in real situations. This will help you improve as you face challenges and build lasting confidence. You are in control of your transformation. You have what it takes to grow your character, one choice at a time. Each decision helps build a strong foundation for success in your career and personal life.

This Book Provides You with Reboot Insights

Chapter 1: Character: Is It Your Greatest Professional Asset? This chapter examines the role of character in professional settings and argues that it may be an individual's most significant asset for achieving success.

Chapter 2: How to Unlock Your Character Database? Readers will learn how to recognize and utilize their unique character traits, which are essential for making a lasting impact in their professional and personal lives.

Chapter 3: Maximizing Your Internal Code. This chapter emphasizes the need to refresh the Character Database to overcome career stagnation and achieve success.

Chapter 4: No Longer on Autopilot: Discovering Your New Operating System. This chapter explores how to transition from a routine lifestyle to one that is more intentional, enabling you to align your actions with your character goals for improved results.

Chapter 5: The Four Pillars of Character: Your Developmental Blueprint This chapter covers the essential elements—Being, Feeling,

Doing, and Becoming—that are crucial for evaluating and shaping one's character.

Chapter 6: The "Being" Pillar: Clean, Life-Sustaining Water. This section examines the Being pillar, emphasizing the relevance of core values and identity in fostering resilience and a robust sense of self, which are crucial for professional development.

Chapter 7: The "Feeling" Pillar: Essential and Unseen Support. This chapter explores the Feeling pillar and provides strategies to enhance emotional intelligence (EI) and relationship skills, both of which are crucial for success in the workplace and for fostering meaningful professional connections.

Chapter 8: The "Doing" Pillar: A Real and Meaningful Environment. Focuses on the Doing pillar, illustrating how to transform personal strengths into tangible actions in the public arena.

Chapter 9: The "Becoming" Pillar: Energetic and Progressively Moving Forward. The text emphasizes the importance of adaptability and vision in the Becoming Pillar, illustrating how they contribute to ongoing growth and staying relevant in your profession.

Chapter 10: Your Character OS Tune-Up Manual: Live the Life! This chapter provides a thorough guide to maintaining an effective and adaptable personal character system over time.

Chapter 11: Your Game is the Long Game. This book concludes by emphasizing the importance of continuous personal growth and character development for enduring success and happiness.

Appendix One: The Historical Perspectives and Ancient Wisdom Behind Character OS. Appendix One examines the historical and ancient origins of character, providing a historical perspective on its enduring significance.

Appendix Two: Modern Character OS: From Science to Practical Applications. Appendix Two bridges current scientific research with real-world applications in character development, establishing a connection between theory and practice.

In Conclusion

This guide is your roadmap. This is a clear and practical guide to fundamentally changing your character, not just a mix of motivational quotes or unclear concepts. It is not a set list of dos and don'ts. You'll leverage strengths already in your Character Database, apply practical steps (not platitudes), and align daily actions to what matters most. You'll work the Four Pillars—Being, Feeling, Doing, and Becoming—to upgrade from autopilot to intentional and peak performance leadership. In a world crowded with technical skill and AI models, your character is the differentiator. Reading Character OS for Professionals will facilitate a Character OS Reboot for most professionals. A Personal Companion Workbook is available to facilitate implementation and application. Also available is Dr. A's Character Workshop online course for those with stubborn liabilities who need additional assistance to recover lost assets and remove or neutralize persistent liabilities. Scan the QR code at the end of this book for additional Character resources.

Think of it as your tech support team. You will have the opportunity to identify the internal challenges that may be holding you back. You may drop the distractions that are hindering your progress. Make new improvements in feelings, ethics, and behavior. Plan your day around what matters to you. When you enhance your Character OS, you unlock your full potential. You create a path that succeeds and feels rewarding, and you make a lasting impact that motivates others to follow in your footsteps.

And here's the most exciting part before you get started: You can begin with something already in place. You own everything you need within your Character Database.

This guide reveals the steps to enhance it—section by section, one choice at a time. Every part provides quick steps and profound understanding to help you reset with purpose and focus. In a landscape filled with technical ability, your unique persona sets you apart. Are you prepared? Let's do this!

Benjamín Alicea-Lugo, PhD

*"Whether everyone is watching, or no one is watching, I owe it to myself **to be, to feel, to do, and to become** my very best self."*

CHAPTER 1

CHARACTER: IS IT YOUR GREATEST PROFESSIONAL ASSET?

Stevie Wonder

"Ability may get you to the top, but it takes character to keep you there."

Squaring the Circle

Why Your Career Has Stalled and What to Do About It

You are reading this because something is not quite right. Your progress, which was once consistent and steady, has now come to a halt. Your hard work isn't yielding the progress you had hoped for anymore. You sense that your visibility is diminishing, and your career has shipwrecked. This can lead to a sense of stagnation in your career, where you feel disregarded and undervalued.

You possess ambitious aspirations and diligently strive to realize them in your professional life. If you are a young leader looking to grow, a manager dealing with challenges, or an experienced executive with many successes, you have worked hard. You have invested countless hours and considerable effort into your career. You have developed your technical skills, created valuable connections, and worked hard to earn promotions.

You may have encountered the word "character" in various contexts. It pops up in corporate mission statements, leadership seminars, and even casual conversations. People sometimes highlight it as a crucial component of success. In a business world that focuses heavily on measurable metrics, such as marketing ROI, quarterly earnings, and sales growth, the concept of character can seem vague and difficult to define. Defining it can be tough, measuring it presents challenges, and in the face of constant pressure to achieve quick results, it is all too easy to overlook it.

This is a significant mistake, and you likely have an opinion about it. You sense the real bottleneck isn't a lack of a new productivity hack, a different networking strategy, or the presence of AI. It's the outcome of something more profound and internal. Many capable professionals unknowingly run on what can be called EgoOS: a default operating system built to ascend through comparison and fear, which explains why they hit an invisible ceiling. You're starting to see that the problem lies within this internal system, and the solution is to upgrade to a new Character OS. This is the core code that shapes traits like discipline, integrity, courage, resilience, humility, and accountability. This internal system is complex to see. It is often referred to as a "soft skill." This label downplays its importance. It can lead capable people like you to overlook the key to lasting success. This misconception precisely explains why so many professionals encounter an invisible ceiling, unable to identify the underlying cause of their stagnation.

Today, we live in a competitive world. Artificial intelligence and automation are taking over many routine tasks. Your character is what makes you human, and it sets you apart from other people and things. Your ability to maintain peak performance will support you not only in your current job but also in future industries and throughout your entire career journey. Neglecting it means risking the very professional momentum you're fighting to regain. To break free from this cycle, you need to do some inner work. This begins with clearly distinguishing character from its often-confused cousins: personality and reputation. This difference isn't just about words. It's the first crucial step required for a character-driven transformation that leads to lasting success.

Character, Personality, and Reputation

What's the Difference?

To fix a problem, you need to understand it first. For the stalled professional, confusion between character, personality, and reputation can mask the trustworthy source of the career bottleneck.

Your reputation is essentially how others see you and what they believe about you. Your reputation depends on what you do, what you accomplish, and how you act in public. However, incomplete information or the biases of those observing you can cloud this view. For instance, you could be known as the person everyone turns to when it comes to successfully closing complicated deals. However, if reaching those goals means pushing aside coworkers, keeping information to oneself, or bending the rules, then that reputation is just resting on a weak base. As a professional who feels stuck, you may have felt frustrated by seeing your peers, who seem to have fewer skills, move ahead. This is often due to their reputation for being reliable, collaborative, and trustworthy. The absence of these traits may be hindering your progress.

Your personality, in contrast, reflects your natural tendencies and the patterns you have for thinking, feeling, and behaving that are inherent to you. Personality frameworks such as the Big Five (see Appendix Two for more information), which include Openness, Conscientiousness, Extraversion, Agreeableness, and Neuroticism, serve to outline these qualities and offer information regarding self-awareness. If your personality is friendly and sociable, you could shine at networking and building relationships. An introverted and detail-oriented professional can create precise, flawless work but may struggle to motivate their team or advocate for their ideas.

Personality is what you present to the world; it is your outward expression of yourself. But it doesn't, by itself, guarantee sustained momentum. For professionals who feel trapped, this crucial insight reveals that simply recognizing your natural style is insufficient to explain why the career advice you've followed has failed to reignite your status. Personality traits are mostly stable. Positive psychology research suggests that it is possible to cultivate and enhance these traits. Intentional character development can lead to this improvement in personality.

Character transcends both. It is the bedrock beneath personality and the trustworthy source of a lasting reputation. It is the integrated sum of your values, ethics, and moral commitments—the core of who you are. Character isn't just about how others see you. It's about the choices you make. These choices should be principled. They matter most when no one is watching. They become significant when the stakes are elevated. They matter most when it's hard to do the right thing.

Character Runs Deeper

Character isn't forged in a single, heroic moment of crisis. It is cultivated and revealed in the countless small, seemingly mundane decisions you make every single day in the professional trenches. When your project goes off track, do you quickly accept responsibility for the mistakes, or do you try to shift the blame to safeguard your reputation? When presented with an effortless solution, such as manipulating numbers in a report to achieve immediate success, do you choose to adhere to your principles? Or do you take the easier path? The decisions we make shape our Being identity. Everyday challenges help you stay true to your values. They come up when temptation, pride, or convenience tries to lead you off your path.

Some people work hard and possess excellent skills, yet still feel stuck. Often, it is the little choices they make that hold them back. When a person makes the wrong ethical choices, skips tough conversations, or prioritizes their pride over the team's success, it can slowly erode their trustworthiness. This behavior can lead to a loss of trust. It can also slow down their career growth over time. Building character does not require a grand display. It comes from the quiet strength you show after facing rejection. It's about the humility you have when you recognize your team's efforts. It's also about the discipline you keep in finishing a challenging project. This depth is what distinguishes temporary victories from lasting success. They turn individual accomplishments into a career path that yields increasing benefits over time. If you notice that your progress, which used to be steady, has slowed or come to a stop, it's a clear sign that it's time to upgrade your Character OS. You need to work on developing the traits that enable you to act consistently and with purpose.

The Bedrock of Your Career Success

Your Character OS

Your Character OS serves as the fundamental software that drives every aspect of your professional life. It works quietly behind the scenes, influencing the way you absorb information, make decisions, manage stress, and interact with your coworkers. Your skills, including your industry knowledge, strategic thinking, and technical expertise, function like the applications that operate on this system. They are powerful and necessary. But even the most sophisticated apps will crash, lag, or produce errors if the operating system is buggy, unstable, or insecure. Some talented professionals fail. Although their "apps" are excellent, their OS is flawed. Ego, dishonesty, or a lack of accountability corrupts the situation. This erodes trust and destroys opportunities.

Your technical skills and expertise—your "apps"—are what got you this far. To break through to the next level of performance and influence, you must undergo a system-level reboot of your character, which is not just beneficial but essential. As you progress in your career, the importance of character increasingly surpasses that of raw technical skills. In a crowded job market, many candidates have similar skills. What makes you stand out is your character. In the age of AI, your reliability, ethics, and ability to lead are what make you truly valuable. This is the reset you have been looking for: a practical, evidence-informed path to rebuild your core traits. It will restore your focus and follow-through, reclaiming your influence.

Practical Proof

Persona in Motion

Who has influenced history through the example of exceptional character content? Let's take a look at a few notable figures.

Dolly Parton is a performer and musician. Theme parks, fantastic music, and her glitzy appearance have made her a famous personality. She is a committed professional with strong principles, hidden beneath all the glitter. Her generosity, especially with the Imagination Library, has made a big difference in the lives of many children. She is loyal, humble, and always ready to help others. She works tirelessly to create a positive impact. Her character goes much deeper than her public image suggests and is often overlooked in the glitz and the glamour.

Keanu Reeves is a well-known actor recognized for his memorable performances in action movies like John Wick and The Matrix. Crew members have reported that he treats everyone on set with respect, regardless of their role. Even in the absence of cameras, people admire him for his modesty, generosity, friendliness, and approachability. Because his character content is so unconventional and unexpected for a Hollywood actor, it often goes viral. Keanu has overcome profound personal tragedies, including the loss of a child and a partner.

According to **Warren Buffett**, also known as the "Oracle of Omaha," personal integrity is an asset that grows in importance over time. Buffett emphasized the importance of honesty, humility, and long-term thinking in a sector that often prioritizes short-term profits and unethical practices. "It takes twenty years to build a reputation but just five to destroy it," he declared. Investors appreciate his intelligence and reliability. His Character OS engenders emotional and financial investment in people and by people.

Aaron Judge exemplifies genuine leadership through his unwavering character as the Captain of the New York Yankees. He attributes his work ethic and moral compass to his adoptive parents. Throughout his meteoric rise from the minor leagues to an outstanding first season in MLB, his modesty and talent were evident. Despite his numerous achievements, he remains adept at sharing the spotlight with his teammates. When pressure mounts, Captain Judge takes charge. The impact of his All Rise Foundation is expanding well beyond the realm of sports.

The Rev. Dr. Justo L. González has dedicated his life to exploring and explaining the vibrant history of Hispanic and Latino Christianity. He's a skilled and active writer, historian, and theologian. "A History of Christian Thought" and "The Story of Christianity" are two of his seminal works, considered essential reading for theologians worldwide. Among Cubans and other Latinos, as well as beyond, he is an inspiration for his leadership, intelligence, and far-reaching contributions.

Tennis star **Roger Federer** is renowned for his consistent play, poise, honesty, and professionalism throughout his illustrious career. In addition to guiding younger players and calmly handling setbacks, he has donated millions to African education through his foundation. The focus is often on his athletic accomplishments, and should also be on his character and humanitarian efforts.

The Growth Imperative

Character Can Be Developed

One of the most empowering truths in this whole discussion is that character is not a fixed or innate trait. Childhood is not a fixed period. Your character can change. It will evolve and grow over time. It is like exercising to become stronger or practicing to improve a skill. This concept directly challenges the myth that people are incapable of change. Holding onto this belief can create a sense of hopelessness, especially when you discover yourself feeling trapped.

Psychologists Christopher Peterson and Martin Seligman have made significant contributions by identifying globally recognized virtues and character strengths (see Appendix Two for more information). These include qualities like bravery, kindness, fairness, curiosity, and wisdom. These traits are valued in various cultures and can be intentionally cultivated to improve both professional effectiveness and personal satisfaction. New studies in neuroscience and psychology demonstrate that our brains can change and adapt throughout our lives, including as we age. We can build new neural pathways by practicing consistently and with purpose. These practices include mindfulness, ethical reflection, and the formation of disciplined habits.

For you, the stalled professional, this is a profoundly hopeful message. Stuckness is not a permanent state. Deciding to start a Character Reboot is not a sign of weakness; instead, it shows great strength, self-awareness, and a strong dedication to creating a meaningful career and lasting legacy. Your journey begins with a genuine self-examination and a commitment to adopt a growth mindset. Instead of seeing your current challenges as obstacles, view them as the beginning of your most important professional transformation.

The Multiplier Effect of Character Assets

A strong Character OS does not just enhance your professional skills; it significantly boosts the effectiveness of everything else you know and do in meaningful ways.

1. **Trust Acceleration:** Character fosters authentic trust rapidly. In a professional setting, trust serves as a key factor, facilitating smooth interactions, minimizing defensive behavior, and enhancing teamwork. Colleagues are more willing to cooperate and innovate when they understand that you lead with integrity. This is crucial for breaking through stagnation that stems from relational breakdowns or a lack of political capital.

2. **Crisis Leadership**: In times of crisis or setbacks, individuals seek support beyond spreadsheets. They are looking for a leader instead. Your technical skills can find a solution. Your character is what truly counts. Your calmness, bravery, and honesty build trust. They ease worries and encourage others to support you and the common task.

3. **Long-Term Value Creation:** Leaders who prioritize character also value long-term success. They avoid pursuing quick wins that might be deceptive. This thoughtful and progressive approach will take some time and effort, but it ultimately yields significant career advantages. It helps you establish a strong reputation and create a body of work that endures over the years. This provides a strong solution for the letdown you feel when your hard work doesn't show results right away.

4. **Genuine Impact and Influence:** In today's workplace, which is increasingly collaborative and interconnected, simply holding a title is not sufficient to earn influence. People are realizing that actual impact comes from building relationships and working together, rather than just relying on their job position. It comes from being genuinely present. The essence of authenticity comes from character. It earns respect and attracts people to

you, enabling you to make a genuine difference that extends beyond your title within the organization.

5. **Improved Ability to Adjust:** Having a strong character helps you adapt and bounce back when you face challenging situations. It helps develop traits like bravery and determination. These traits allow you to handle difficult situations effectively. Resilience is crucial for driving innovation and maintaining high performance in a rapidly evolving economy. It is a key part of any successful career restart.

Character OS Consequences for Your Professional Future

If your character is your best asset, develop it as much as your strategic or technical skills. Here are the ways to maximize character content:

1. **Incorporate Personal Character Into Your Professional Growth Strategy:** Simply obtaining credentials in your field or enrolling in leadership programs is not sufficient. Include character introspection in your daily schedule. Just as you learn to use a new piece of software, you should work on developing assets like patience, honesty, and responsibility.

2. **Make Decisions Based on Character:** Always ask yourself, "What fits with who I want to be?" when faced with a critical or difficult decision. When circumstances break down, a person's character shines through.

3. **Cultivate a Strong Character for Elevated Leadership**: Your character will receive greater attention and power as you advance in your career. If you invest in it, the culture you build will attract followers and promotion.

4. **Create a Lasting Legacy:** Possessing character assets unlocks new opportunities. The power to be consistent lies in its ability to establish trust, strengthen relationships, and leave a lasting impression. Adherence to one's principles, rather than perfection, is what matters.

In Conclusion

If character is indeed your most significant professional asset, then its development deserves the same strategic focus and dedicated effort you apply to your technical and leadership skills. This involves going beyond simply obtaining another certification or attending another seminar. It consists of integrating character development into the foundation of your professional growth plan.

Schedule regular "character audits" with the same level of seriousness as a financial review. Practice patience, accountability, and empathy with the same discipline you would use to master a new piece of software. For you, the ambitious professional ready for a change, this is the path from stagnation to sustained peak performance. It is about taking your core values and turning them into daily actions. These actions lead to strong results. Investing in your Character OS is a powerful choice. It can help break the barriers that hold you back. This choice can spark your career and allow you to create a lasting legacy of success and purpose.

Key Takeaways

1. Character is your professional operating system. Your Character OS influences everything in your work life, from how you absorb information and make decisions to how you manage stress and interact with coworkers.

2. Character differs from personality and reputation. Your character reflects your core values and the choices you make, especially when no one is watching. On the other hand, your personality reflects your innate tendencies, and how others perceive you shapes your reputation.

3. Everyday choices shape who we are. It develops through various small professional choices—embracing responsibility, opting for integrity over shortcuts, and prioritizing team success over personal pride.

4. Character flaws and career setbacks usually arise from issues beyond just a lack of skills. Ego, dishonesty, and a lack of accountability can undermine even the most skilled professionals, underscoring the importance of character development for achieving lasting success.

5. A strong character enhances your professional impact. Character builds trust, boosts leadership credibility, and leaves a lasting professional impact that goes beyond just technical skills.

Thomas Edison

"What a man's mind can create, man's character can control."

CHAPTER 2

How to Unlock Your Character Database?

Billy Graham:

"The greatest legacy one can pass on to one's children and grandchildren is not money or other material things accumulated in one's life, but rather a legacy of character and faith."

Your Internal Operating System

As you read this, a hidden system is working inside you. You did not create it, but it is one of the strongest forces shaping your everyday life. This system operates diligently in the background. It affects every choice, word, and action you make, often without you even knowing.

Just as your smartphone depends on its operating system to run applications, send messages, and process commands, your character operates through what I call your Character Database—an intricate internal framework that stores and processes. It influences every aspect of who you are and how you show up in the world.

Think of this database as your mission control center. Your mind takes in everything from your daily life. It absorbs what you see, hear, think, feel, and experience. Then, it turns this data into outputs that shape your actions, reactions, habits, and reputation. This truly human system tracks your thoughts, words, attitudes, and behaviors. It builds a detailed picture of who you are.

Knowing your current Character Database is not just helpful; it is crucial for anyone who wants to grow personally and achieve real success. This is the key to achieving meaningful goals. It helps you find more satisfaction in life. If you are not familiar with your Character Database content, you will likely feel confused. Have you ever thought about why something keeps happening in your life? Or why do you sometimes feel disconnected from what you are doing?

Your Database Can Work For You

Your Character Database can be invaluable. It's like a trustworthy friend you can rely on. Your core values and beliefs are always present for you. They serve as a guide when you're uncertain about your path. When you face a tough choice, you want to be able to trust the inner guidance that comes from it. Your experiences, values, and the wisdom you have accumulated over time shape this guidance.

Your database is like a personal reference guide. It helps you remember what makes you unique and vital. If someone asks about your strengths, values, or what you believe in, this system enables you to express your identity clearly and confidently. This inner ally affects how you react to daily events. It also guides you in making important life choices.

Perhaps most importantly, a well-functioning Character Database creates consistency and reliability in your interactions with others. People begin to know what to expect from you because your responses align with your stated values. Being consistent helps build trust and strengthen relationships. It allows you to stay true to yourself in various situations and with different people.

When Your Database Betrays You

Your Character Database can also be a formidable obstacle. The system that helps you succeed can also create self-limiting beliefs and detrimental habits. These obstacles can prevent you from achieving your full potential. Your database holds more than just your strengths and positive traits. It also keeps track of your weaknesses, insecurities, fears, and all the negative patterns you have formed.

Problems start when your internal system has conflicting information. Your database may urge you to be kind and helpful, but it also tells you to stay safe. It can motivate you to take significant risks, but it can also instill fear of failure or rejection. Occasionally, these internal contradictions happen without you being conscious of them. Your actions can sometimes seem random. You may find these concepts challenging to grasp fully.

The Character Mess: When Contradictions Take Control

The biggest issue happens when you create what I call a "character mess." You can feel it inside, and others can see it outside. This occurs when your database is filled with conflicting character assets and liabilities, and regrettably, the liabilities have taken the lead.

If you're not regularly engaging in self-reflection and conscious character development, you might not immediately recognize this inner chaos. The symptoms are often evident. You may observe behavior that is confusing and frustrating to those around you. You experience a significant amount of emotional stress. It can wear you out. You may continue to encounter the same relationship issues. They can feel like they follow you around.

One day, you're kind and caring. The next day, you feel defensive and want to protect yourself. You awaken with a sense of confidence and capability, yet in the afternoon, insecurity and self-doubt consume you. You make sincere promises to keep them, then observe yourself unable or unwilling to follow through.

This pattern of inconsistency creates confusion. It affects not only those around you but also you internally. You begin to feel disconnected from what you chose and did. It feels like someone else is in charge of your choices.

If you continue to avoid self-reflection and focus on improving your character, you may become what I call a "perpetual contradiction." This means others will perceive it as challenging to read you or understand what to expect. You also won't fully understand yourself or be someone on whom you can rely. Colleagues might say, "I never know which version of you I'm going to get," while family members express their frustration: "You're so inconsistent—I can't count on you."

How Your Database Loads Up

Understanding Human Inputs

Your Character Database was not built overnight. It is formed through a series of human inputs that continue to shape you throughout your life. Let us explore the three input sources.

Input Source #1: Your Genetic Foundation

Your personality and genetics are foundational input sources. They are your biological starting point and can't be changed fundamentally. Let's call these your "factory settings." It's crucial to understand that, despite the unchangeable nature of this foundation, it need not impede your growth and transformation.

From the moment you were born, you possessed specific personality traits that were already a part of you. You might be naturally introverted or extroverted, optimistic or cautious, and analytical or intuitive. These represent your default settings—the automatic patterns that influence how you naturally express your character and interact with the world around you.

Your genetic makeup determines fundamental aspects of how you process information, handle stress, connect with other people, and manage change and challenges. You cannot change your DNA. However, you can learn to work with it and improve some of its outcomes.

Your natural inclinations should not hold you back. They help you build your character and grow as a person. Understanding your genetic personality can provide you with insight into the traits that come naturally to you. It indicates areas where you may want to put in more effort and attention.

A cautious person can still become very brave and bold. A person who acts on impulse can learn to be patient and think things through carefully. Everyone's journey will be different, but anyone ready to put in the effort can experience genuine character change. You can still be you (personality and DNA) and build upon it.

Input Source #2: How Society and Environment Shape Us

Your family and primary caregivers are usually the first and most powerful influences on who you become. They help shape your character as you grow up. Your caregivers and family did not just provide you with food, shelter, and love; they also gave you a sense of belonging and a sense of purpose. They demonstrated the importance of character and values, as well as how to navigate relationships and face challenges.

Your family taught you your first ideas of right and wrong. They shaped your views on kindness and cruelty. You learned what strength and vulnerability mean. You also experienced love, acceptance, conflict, and rejection in relation to strength and vulnerability.

Every family dinner became a classroom for character development. Every moment of discipline, celebration, or crisis becomes a lesson. It teaches us about values, priorities, and handling life's complexities. The way your parents managed stress demonstrated how to handle pressure and adversity. The way they handled money influenced your early views on finances, success, and feelings of security. The way they treated others—family, neighbors, and service workers—shaped your first ideas about respect, relationships, and human dignity.

Your family taught you about both good and negative relationship patterns. You noticed both the good and adverse ways people interact. Your early experiences shaped who you are. They shaped your expectations and reactions for a long time. But what if your early family input was inadequate, inconsistent, or harmful? The encouraging news is that your childhood social conditioning, regardless of its quality, remains accessible in your database as raw material for growth. You are still determining the role these early influences play in your current life. Understanding their ongoing impact becomes a crucial starting point in any serious Character Reboot process. The critical review of your early childhood database may require therapeutic help to sort out and process. In the absence of this formal help, self-help and reflection with caregivers can provide valuable assistance.

Social conditioning extends far beyond your immediate family. Your school experiences, community, religious or social institutions, cultural organizations, and friends all play a part in this. All these sources helped shape who you are. They influenced your values and what you consider acceptable behavior.

Sometimes, these different influences supported the values you learned at home. This created a sense of consistency and clarity. Occasionally, they created conflict, confusion, or even contradictions. This made it challenging to understand what it means to reflect character excellence. As you grow older, you begin to question and reevaluate the lessons you learned in your early years. You start to think carefully about what to keep, what to change, and what to let go of completely. You can either stick to your old habits or make fundamental changes in your life.

Input Source #3: Experience and Understanding of Life

The third primary input source is what I refer to as experiential data. This includes what you believe and how you see life events, relationships, successes, and failures. Your identity is shaped by more than just your experiences. It is about how you understand and process your experiences. It is about the meaning you give them.

Two people can experience the same events but emerge with quite different perceptions. Why is that? Their interpretations, beliefs, and processes of meaning-making exhibit significant differences. Your experiences shape your thoughts and what you believe. Your choices and habits shape who you become. They are all connected and defining.

When we handle positive experiences effectively, they can help us grow and improve. They develop key traits like resilience, confidence, humility, and empathy. Negative experiences can change us in other ways. They can help us build valuable traits like perseverance and wisdom. On the other hand, they can also lead to issues such as cynicism, insecurity, defensiveness, and a lack of empathy towards others.

As time goes on, these patterns deposited in your Character Database build up and deepen. They change how you react to familiar situations and new challenges. Your past experiences shape your present and future character content. But you can change this cycle. By being aware and making intentional choices, you can take control of your life.

The Evolution of Your Database

Here's a fundamental truth about character development: while your genetic makeup establishes the initial and ongoing framework, you are never a completed project. You are like a book that is always being written. Your Character Database continually changes and grows as you progress through various stages and experiences in life.

As you become more aware of yourself, you gain new experiences and meet different people. This helps your understanding change and grow. As children, we take in character traits without much thought. Over time, we start to choose and shape those traits more actively.

This transition—from unconsciously absorbing character data to deliberately choosing what to embrace—represents a crucial turning point in personal maturity and development. As a child, you accepted character lessons without question, assuming they existed as is. As a mature adult, you develop the capacity to evaluate, choose, and decide what serves you and what holds you back.

One of life's most empowering transitions involves moving from caregiver influence to authentic self-governance. Your early role models helped shape you, but ultimately, you are the principal owner of your character content.

The Never-Ending Information Stream Challenge

In today's connected world, you get a lot of new character information. Some of it is helpful and positive, while other parts can be harmful and limiting. Much of it can also be confusing and contradictory.

You get character-related content from many places every day—some of it you notice, and some of it you don't.

Think about the different influences on your character. These include family, friends, romantic partners, and acquaintances. Work colleagues in a professional setting also play a role. Please keep in mind social media, entertainment, television, radio, podcasts, and online content.

These information streams never pause or slow down—and they frequently contradict each other. Your workplace culture might reward ruthless competition and self-promotion. Your friends might make lying, gossiping, or taking easy ways out seem normal. Popular media frequently celebrate narcissism. It emphasizes immediate gratification and superficial achievements. Your inner values and more profound wisdom may lead you to different ways of living and connecting with others.

This creates an ongoing dilemma that every thoughtful person must navigate: Will the newly acquired information enhance or corrupt your character? Every piece of information you absorb has a cumulative effect—it either adds valuable assets to your Character Database or compounds its existing liabilities.

The principle is straightforward: garbage in, garbage out. Assets in, assets out. Liabilities come in, liabilities go out. The things you let into your database shape who you are. They influence your character and how you act. This is why it is vital to protect and nurture your Character Database in today's fast-paced world.

To succeed and stay true to yourself, you need to be an active gatekeeper. This means filtering what you let in, asking questions, and carefully choosing the character data you assimilate into your life. You cannot afford to be passive—you must function as the system administrator or the gatekeeper of your Character Operating System.

How Your Database Shows Off

Your Character Database is not a quiet or hidden system that works in total secrecy. It is evident in three main areas. Your actions show who you really are to everyone around you. They are observable, measurable, and undeniable.

Output Category #1: Your Thoughts and Inner Voice

Your thoughts are like a steady flow of ideas and opinions. Your thoughts fluctuate as you navigate through your daily experiences. This includes your inner thoughts—the conversation you have with yourself. What you say to yourself in the shower to the committee known as "me, myself and I." It also covers how you perceive and interpret the world around you.

Your Character Database acts like a strong filter. It shapes how you think by linking your values, beliefs, and experiences to your perception of the present. You can share some of these thoughts with others. But many stay private, and they shape your mental landscape.

If your database has traits like optimism, gratitude, and faith in others, you often think about hope and appreciation. You see the potential for good things to happen. You will begin to see the good energy around you more clearly. You'll see potential even in challenging situations. You will also have faith in the best intentions and abilities of others.

If resentment, cynicism, or fear takes over your thoughts and your inner voice, it will always reflect those negative views. You'll struggle to believe in positive outcomes or trust other people's intentions, and your mind will automatically default to suspicion, sarcasm, and self-doubt.

Your thoughts function as the internal voice of your character, affecting your worldview, personal reflections, and subsequent actions—even when no one else can hear them. They create the mental environment in which you live every day, either supporting your growth and happiness or undermining your potential and peace of mind.

Output Category #2: Your Actions and Behaviors

Your actions show who you are. They include everything you say and do. Others can see and judge these expressions of your character. Your actions reflect your free will and the influence of society on you. They are clear proof of your true self.

Actions are different from thoughts. They are visible to others. This shows your true character, which everyone can notice and judge. Your thoughts might be hidden, but your actions show who you are. They shape your reputation and influence how others perceive you in both personal and professional relationships.

Occasionally, you might see that what you do does not match what you say you want or who you want to be. Despite your best efforts to remain patient, you often discover yourself losing your patience. You want to be generous and giving. But when faced with challenges, you frequently act selfishly. These contradictions are helpful clues that you are storing conflicting or unclear character information in your database.

If your internal values are unclear or conflicting, your behavior on the outside can become inconsistent and unpredictable. People around you find it difficult to predict which version of you they will see each day. Your actions matter a lot. They shape your reputation and affect how others see you in a relationship. People may eventually forget what you claimed to believe or the impressive things you said about yourself, but they will never forget how you made them feel through your concrete behaviors and treatment of them.

The goal is to let your actions consistently communicate the best aspects of your Character Database rather than its dysfunctions and contradictions.

Output Category #3: Your Attitudes and Mental Postures

How often have you heard someone say, "You need to adjust your attitude!" Attitudes represent your long-standing mental positions—your default settings about life, other people, and yourself that have been reinforced and solidified over time. Attitudes differ from fleeting feelings or shifting opinions. They last longer and consistently reflect your thoughts based on your knowledge.

Attitudes possess a unique stability that distinguishes them from both temporary thoughts and unchangeable personality traits. They stay the same for a long time, or until you say, "Enough!" This creates patterns in how you confront life's challenges. Unlike core genetic traits, attitudes can change. With effort and awareness, we can modify them.

Your attitudes reflect the wisdom you have gained and the wounds you still carry from your life experiences. Your experiences shape how you interact with authority, manage finances, build relationships, navigate work challenges, and perceive success or failure in your life.

Your attitudes are the key connection between what you think and how you act. They help create a consistent and predictable pattern. They influence your expectations of others, your perspective on situations, and your overall satisfaction with life.

A person who values traits like humility, gratitude, and openness will likely seek opportunities to grow, learn, and collaborate in various situations. A person who has experienced scarcity and distrust may anticipate betrayal, competition, and disappointment in every situation.

Your attitudes shape the link between your inner beliefs and your outward behavior. This connection affects every significant relationship and decision you make.

The Complexity Factor

As you age, your Character Database gets more complex. This feels somewhat normal. Life can be tough, constantly throwing new experiences, influences, and challenges our way. Every challenge needs you to think more carefully. Your Character Database grows and changes with each new deposit.

A longer life creates a bigger database. This can lead to more conflicting information. You may have beliefs from your childhood that conflict with your understanding as an adult. You may hold cultural or religious values that do not match your current beliefs. Your work life may push you to act in ways that do not align with your values.

Consider this example: two brothers grow up in the same household. They share the same inputs: genetics, social conditioning, and experiences. But they end up quite different. Why is that? Each brother's Character Database grows through a personal and unique filtering process. This shows that even if the inputs are almost identical, our processing differs, and therefore so do the outcomes.

In Conclusion

You are not stuck with the factory settings. You have a chance to take control of your inner world. Take charge of your Character Database. This is not about removing your past. It's like being the editor of a story you're still writing. To become the person you wish to be, you must control your story. You can evaluate your character content. Decide what to keep, what to update, and what to let go. This is your chance to create character content that feels real and true to you. Your Character OS can either be your greatest ally or your greatest adversary. When it works well, it serves as a reliable internal compass, helping you stay true to yourself.

Key Takeaways

1. **Your Character Database is your inner operating system and stores your character content.** Your character is like a secret part of you. Your thoughts, habits, and values are stored there. They help you make decisions every day. Knowing it is your first big step toward growing on purpose.

2. **The two sides of your database:** Your character content can be your greatest ally, helping you gain the trust of others. But they can also point out your flaws and lead to confusing behaviors for everyone, including yourself.

3. **Where it all comes from:** Your database is built from three main sources: your natural personality and genetics, lessons from family and society, and how your understanding of life. These factors continue to shape who you are.

4. **Taking charge over time**: As you get older, you stop just taking in everything around you and start choosing what you want to keep, kind of like being the boss of your system to fit your goals and values.

5. **How it shows up in life:** Your thoughts, actions, and attitudes shape your relationships and how others view you. They also affect your happiness, so try to align them for a better experience.

Heraclitus of Ephesus:

"Good character is not formed in a week or a month. It is created little by little, day by day. Protracted and patient effort is needed to develop good character."

CHAPTER 3

MAXIMIZING YOUR INTERNAL CODE

Anonymous

"The short-term pain of accepting a truth is far better than the long-term pain of believing an illusion."

Understanding How You Work Inside

Here's what most career advice won't tell you: The main issue does not lie in your resume, networking skills, or technical abilities. It's your internal operating system—what we call your Character Database—that controls how you think, act, and respond in professional situations.

Think of your professional life like a smartphone. It's great to download all the best apps (skills and knowledge), but nothing will work properly if your operating system is outdated or broken. Your phone freezes, crashes, or performs poorly. That's precisely what happens to capable professionals who feel stuck despite having impressive credentials.

Your Character Database is like your phone's operating system. It operates quietly in the background. It shapes your decisions, affects your relationships, and guides the opportunities you chase or ignore. When this internal system is functioning correctly, everything flows smoothly. When this internal system isn't functioning properly, even your most diligent efforts can feel like a daunting task.

How Your Professional Character Got Programmed

The Caregiver Stage: Your First Programming

As stated in the previous chapter, your professional character didn't start forming when you got your first job. It began much earlier, during what we call the caregiver stage of your development.

As a child and teenager, the adults around you—like parents, teachers, and coaches—were shaping your character without you even knowing it. They chose which behaviors would be rewarded and which would be punished. Your experiences taught you what hard work, success, and positive relationships mean.

You absorbed these lessons without intending to. If your parents praised you for perfect grades, you might think that anything less is not good enough. If a teacher praised you for sticking to the rules, you might think that challenging authority is dangerous. If a coach focused on individual achievements instead of team success, you learned that personal performance is more important than working together.

Your early experiences shaped your default settings. We can call this default programming EgoOS—an operating system built on a simple, brutal architecture: ascend. It runs silently in the background of our lives, fueled by comparison and constantly running threat assessments against our status. These are the automatic responses and behaviors that continue to influence your actions in professional situations today. Regardless of whether you are 35, 45, or 55 years old, that early programming continues to impact your career choices.

The Problem with Default Settings

The challenge is that strategies that benefited you as a child or young adult may now be hindering your career. You might have been taught to follow directions without question. However, today's workplace needs you to take initiative and show leadership. You may have learned that being overly confident is perceived as a form of showing off. But in your current role, you need to have a strong presence and make bold decisions.

You have probably been taught that hard work leads to success. However, you now see that building relationships and influencing others is just as crucial as working independently and being productive. You might have learned to avoid conflict. To advance in your career, you sometimes have to have hard talks and stand up for your ideas.

These internal contradictions lead to character conflicts. This happens when your ingrained beliefs clash with what you need to succeed at work. It is like trying to run new software on an old computer. The EgoOS, which pings servers for social approval and displays pop-up notifications of self-promotion, is incompatible with modern collaborative environments. Its background scripts of fear—fear of being overlooked, of being average, of insignificance—directly cause the career stagnation you feel. The conflict creates tension. It leads to confusion and mixed results.

Understanding Your Character Conflicts

If you have been in any of these situations, you are dealing with character conflicts.

- You know you should share your ideas in meetings. Still, you often stay quiet.
- You want to take on challenging projects. But you often hesitate.
- You know networking is essential. Still, you avoid professional events.
- You believe in your ideas, but it is challenging for you to share them.

- You want to give away more tasks. But you end up doing everything by yourself.
- You know you need to set boundaries. Still, you keep saying yes to everything.

These are not necessarily flaws or weaknesses. They are signs that your internal operating system needs an update.

The Independence Phase: Taking Control of Your Character Database

Here's the exciting news that can transform your career: You don't have to stay stuck with the character programming you inherited.

As you mature professionally, you move into what we call the independence phase of character development. In this phase, you take charge of creating your character content. You are not stuck with the traits and behaviors you were given when you were younger. Choose your values and practice intentional behaviors. Develop new traits that help you reach your professional goals.

This change from being a passive recipient to actively programming your character sets professionals apart. Those who break through career plateaus do so while others stay stuck in the same autopilot patterns year after year.

The Power of Conscious Choice

When you take control of your Character Database, you must accept this truth: you cannot change your past. But you can shape how you respond in the future.

You did not pick the early programming that influenced who you are today. You can now decide what to keep, what to update, and what to replace in the future. This is empowering but also challenging. It means you are responsible for your professional growth in ways you may not have considered before.

Shifting From Rebellion to Purposeful Growth

Occasionally, when people discover they can change how they think, they want to push back against everything they learned as daughters and sons. They want to reject all the values and behaviors their parents, teachers, or early mentors instilled in them.

Wholesale rebellion is not smart. It is just an unproductive way to react. Getting rid of all the values you grew up with can leave you feeling lost and vulnerable. It's essential to think carefully about what to keep. You want to feel empowered and have a clear direction.

You need discernment instead. Some values from your past are still important. They are worth holding on to and fighting for. Others may be outdated or limiting and require updates. The key is to examine them intentionally and thoughtfully, rather than automatically accepting or rejecting them.

Personal growth requires sorting through the beliefs and behaviors you inherited. This means keeping what still serves you and letting go of what no longer fits your professional goals, personal values, and aspirations.

Understanding Your Current State

Before you can upgrade your Character Database, you need to understand what's currently running in your system. This requires what we call a "character audit"—an honest assessment of your current traits, behaviors, and patterns.

Most people have never taken the time to map out the character traits they consistently display versus the ones that hold them back. They run on autopilot. They react to situations based on their default programming. They are not aware of their character content.

When conducting your character audit, focus on behavior patterns rather than simply good intentions. Think about these questions:

- What do my colleagues and friends often say about me?
- What character traits appear often in my work relationships?
- What patterns show up in my work style or leadership approach?
- What internal challenges keep coming up in various jobs or projects?

These patterns reveal the hidden architecture of your character—both your strengths and your limitations, your character assets and liabilities.

The Three-Part Reboot Process

Once you understand your current character programming, you can begin the transformation process. Character development includes three critical actions that can significantly affect your success at work.

1. Getting Back Lost Professional Assets

The first step is to identify the characteristics of the assets you previously owned. These traits may have been hidden or pushed down over time. Your traits did not vanish; they just got hidden beneath habits that are no longer helpful.

As a child, you might have been curious and asked beneficial questions. But home or school may have taught you that asking questions was a problem. You might have had great creative ideas, but they were suppressed to adhere to the rules. You may have been generous with your time and ideas. But negative experiences taught you to hold back and protect yourself.

Your hidden traits show the potential you have in your career. To recover them, you need to examine your current behaviors closely. Look for the positive qualities that can boost your career effectiveness.

If you were naturally collaborative but learned to work alone to avoid disappointment, you can regain that teamwork spirit while maintaining healthy boundaries. If you used to take the initiative but began to ask for permission after receiving criticism, you can regain your confidence. You can also learn to judge more effectively when to act and in the proper context.

2. Changing Career-Limiting Liabilities

The next step is to find the character traits that are holding you back. Next, consider substituting them with more effective characteristics that suit you.

Every professional has traits that can hinder their success. Procrastination can stop you from starting important projects. Being undisciplined can leave you feeling overwhelmed by too many commitments. Diffidence can hold you back from sharing ideas until they seem "perfect," which often means never sharing them at all. Avoiding conflict can keep you from having meaningful and necessary conversations.

It is important to spot these limiting patterns. Then, you can choose better options on purpose. Procrastination can turn into intelligent prioritization. Being undisciplined can evolve into the practice of setting healthy boundaries. Diffidence can turn into a dedication to doing things well and on time. Conflict avoidance can develop into a skilled and complex form of conversation management.

This replacement process is not just about using willpower to hide negative traits. It is essential to understand why these traits formed. They often had a purpose at some point. Then, we can choose better ways to meet current needs.

3. *Choosing Wisely Each Day*

The third step is about making choices that are consistent and intentional. These choices should align with your professional goals, rather than reverting to old habits.

Character change is not about huge actions or quick wholesale changes. It happens with the little choices we make every day. These choices help build new neural pathways and habits over time.

You make many small choices every day. Your preferences can either reinforce your old habits or help you establish new, healthier ones.

- Will you speak up in the meeting or stay quiet?
- Would you prefer to take on the challenging project or continue with the more manageable tasks?
- Do you prefer to engage in difficult conversations or avoid confrontations?
- Would you prefer to delegate the task or manage it personally?
- Do you set boundaries, or do you consent to all requests?
- Do you share the credit for success, or do you keep it all for yourself?

These daily choices create what psychologists refer to as a "positive feedback loop." Better character choices lead to better professional results, which in turn reinforce your motivation to continue developing your character and enhancing your reputation.

The Relationship Factor in Professional Success

Your Character Database doesn't just affect how you work—it determines how others experience working with you.

In today's collaborative business environment, your ability to build strong professional relationships often matters more than your technical expertise. Companies can train employees on new software, industry knowledge, or specific procedures. However, they can't teach character traits such as trustworthiness, reliability, integrity, and emotional stability.

Character traits like honesty, empathy, loyalty, and confidence form the foundation of deep, lasting professional relationships. Without these traits, working relationships become fragile and transactional—easily damaged when projects become stressful or conflicts arise.

This becomes especially important as you advance in your career. The higher you go in any organization, the more your success depends on your ability to influence others, build coalitions, inspire confidence, and lead teams through challenging situations.

The Business Case for Strong Character

Here's something most career guides won't tell you directly: Character is your ultimate competitive advantage in today's marketplace.

Having technical skills and strong credentials can help you stand out at first. However, it is your character traits that ultimately matter. They decide if you get hired, promoted, trusted with key projects, and given leadership roles.

Why is character important to employers? They know they can teach skills and provide training, but they cannot teach character. Organizations need people who show integrity when things become tough. They should be consistent, ethical, and cooperative.

Character provides a lasting advantage that others cannot easily copy. Competitors can imitate your strategies, match your skills, or even offer better pay packages. They cannot replicate the deep trust, influence, and respect you create by consistently showing good character over time.

This benefit stands out more as markets become tougher and technology makes skills easier to learn. In a world where anyone can quickly learn new software or acquire information, traits like wisdom, judgment, integrity, and people skills stand out.

Creating Influence with Character

A strong character creates what we call "natural influence." This type of leadership does not rely on titles, positions, or formal authority.

Consider the professionals you admire in your field. What attracts you to them? Their achievements may initially capture your attention, but it is their character that earns lasting respect and influence.

These individuals possess what we refer to as "character convictions." These values endure, even when investing elsewhere is easier or more profitable. They make choices based on their values, not just what is expedient.

Being consistent helps build trust and credibility. This can lead to more influence and chances for leadership. People want to work for and with professionals they admire. The students also want to learn from their teachers. Character traits matter.

Natural influence is significant in today's workplace. It goes beyond job titles and organizational charts. Your character-based influence is essential. It helps you lead a project team, collaborate with cross-functional teams, and build client relationships. This influence makes you more effective in any role.

Combining Personality and Character for the Best Results.

Your personality shows your natural tendencies and preferences. It can reveal if you are introverted or extroverted, detail-oriented or focused on the big picture, methodical or spontaneous, and analytical or intuitive. Your traits influence how you prefer to work, absorb information, and interact with others.

Character shows the choices you make, the morals you follow, and the habits you build over time. Your personality usually stays the same as you grow older. However, you can actively develop and improve your character during your career.

The goal is not to conflict with your natural personality traits. This approach can be tiring and may feel inauthentic. The goal is to develop character traits that align with your personality. This will help you grow your professional skills and be more effective.

You can succeed at work without being an extrovert if you're naturally shy. You can build traits like courage and confidence. These help you voice your thoughts when it counts, even if it is tough. If you like to analyze things, you don't have to be spontaneous. But you can work on being adaptable. This will help you adjust when things change suddenly.

Successful professionals achieve a state of "personality-character integration." This means their natural traits blend well with the character traits they have developed. Together, they create absolute professional excellence.

This integration eliminates the exhausting experience of constantly fighting against yourself or pretending to be someone you're not. You become a more complete, adequate, and authentic version of yourself.

Here are some examples of how personality and character can work well together:

- A chatty person who gets wise knows how to share beneficial advice. They strive to create genuine and meaningful dialogue, rather than merely engaging in conversation.
- Having a positive attitude and showing strong empathy can really make a difference for coworkers, helping them feel better and more supported.
- A quiet individual who pays attention can become a go-to source for advice and understanding, among others.
- A person who is naturally analytical and develops humility can become a trusted advisor. They share what they know in a friendly way. They do not act superior or look down on others.

When your personality and character work together rather than against each other, you reduce internal conflict, eliminate mixed signals to others, and can fully leverage both your natural strengths and your developed capabilities.

Your Character Database Serves as a GPS for your Professional Journey

Your Character Database serves as a GPS for making informed career choices. It uses your values and principles to evaluate your current situation and help you plan your path. This way, you can reach meaningful and lasting career goals. This internal navigation system acts as a reliable filter. It helps evaluate opportunities, relationships, challenges, and career moves consistently. Your character traits act like a compass when you face tough decisions. They help you find options that align with your values and goals. This filtering function makes your thinking and decision-making easier. Do not stress about every option or feel overwhelmed by choices. Your

Character Database helps you focus on the best, ethical options that align with your values and support your growth.

Using Character-Based decision-making

This is how character-based decision-making works in everyday jobs:

Evaluating Job Opportunities: Do not just focus on salary and benefits. Ask questions about character expectations: Will this job allow me to showcase my best qualities? Does the company's culture align with my core values? Will I develop both professionally and personally in this environment? Is it necessary for me to compromise my integrity to achieve success here?

Building Professional Relationships: Instead of networking just for your gain, pay attention to assessing character. Can this person be trusted? Do they show honesty? Do they possess character strengths that align well with mine? Will this relationship benefit both of us? Is there an honest exchange of value?

Making Leadership Decisions: As a leader, tough choices come up. Focus on your values. Ask yourself: Which decision benefits everyone the most? How can I balance different interests? What decision will I be happy with in five years? What kind of example am I showing to others?

Managing Career Setbacks: When you confront disappointments or failures, contemplate it this way: What can I learn from this experience? How can I respond while maintaining my integrity and reputation? What traits should I work on to deal with similar situations better next time?

Benefits of Character-Based Navigation Over Time

Character-based decision-making emphasizes long-term excellence over short-term convenience. Occasionally, you have to step back from quick rewards or chances that don't match your values. This method often results in lasting, meaningful, and sustainable success in your career.

This navigation system helps you avoid costly mistakes. It enables you to make choices that improve your professional reputation. You will make better connections. This can lead to new chances for growth and success.

Your character assets serve as a quality control mechanism for your professional life, preserving the integrity of everything you do, say, and choose. Being consistent helps build trust with your colleagues, clients, and supervisors. This trust is key to long-term career success.

In Conclusion

Changing who you are takes more than just wanting to improve or occasionally thinking about it. You need to make consistent and intentional choices. These choices should align with your professional goals, rather than simply following what you have always done.

This is tough and also liberating. It is tough because you have to take complete responsibility for your growth and success in your career. Your past does not have to shape your future. Your current limits can change.

Successful professionals understand that building character is not a one-time endeavor; it is a continuous process. It is an ongoing journey. It takes careful choices, steady actions, and thoughtful reflection.

You can start your career reboot by understanding that you have more control over your future than you realized. Your character is like your guiding light. It shapes your choices, relationships, and everyday actions. It is possible to enhance and refine it so that it aligns more closely with your future aspirations.

Key Takeaways

1. **Get to know your Character Database.** Occasionally, an outdated internal system, or "Character Database," influences your choices and actions, hindering your professional growth, rather than a lack of skills or experience.

2. **Welcome the phase of independence.** Move from being a passive participant in your childhood programming to actively selecting and refining your character traits to match your professional aspirations, freeing yourself from inherited constraints.

3. **Perform a character assessment.** Take a close look at your current traits to identify your strengths (character assets) that you can build on and weaknesses (character liabilities) that you need to address. This approach will enable you to grow purposefully, rather than performing on autopilot.

4. **Make intentional decisions each day.** Character development occurs through a series of small, consistent choices that create new habits and positive feedback loops, ultimately leading to improved professional outcomes.

5. **Make character your key advantage.** Possessing strong character traits like integrity and resilience allows you to naturally impact those around you and foster enduring relationships, distinguishing you in the marketplace beyond mere technical abilities.

Abigail Van Buren:

"The best index to a person's character is how he treats people who can't do him any good."

CHAPTER 4

From Autopilot to Intention: Discovering Your New Operating System

John Zenger

"Great leaders are not defined by the absence of weakness but rather by the presence of clear strengths."

The Character OS Reboot isn't just another self-help concept—it's a complete transformation of who you are at your core. This kind of change reshapes your thoughts, emotions, and behaviors in ways that directly impact your professional success. And here's the best part: it's entirely within your power to make it happen.

You have the choice to let go of the traits that are sabotaging your career—things like arrogance, disorganization, or pessimism. You can replace them with qualities that move the needle: humility, order, and optimism. The ten keys I'm about to share will help you access your Character Database and transform resentment into forgiveness and apathy into passion.

Breaking Free from Career Autopilot

Let's face it—the majority of professionals are unconsciously progressing in their careers. They don't realize that their internal operating system can be updated. Instead, they function like that old computer in your office: once useful, now painfully slow and limiting your potential.

Living on autopilot feels comfortable. It doesn't require effort. You become predictable. You respond without thinking. You act out of habit, reinforcing the same patterns every single day. But think about what that comfort is costing you. It limits your growth. It cuts down on opportunities. Your true self gets buried under habits you don't even notice.

You lose out on your career when you operate passively and are not engaged. You're responding to what others expect or how you were conditioned in the past. It's not about your values or goals. This is why many skilled professionals often feel trapped, despite their knowledge and dedication.

Living intentionally is different. It means being fully present in your professional life. You act with awareness and purpose. You realize that you have the power to change your narrative, beginning at this very moment.

Change begins when we take the time to understand. Pay attention to how you instinctively respond in meetings, when conflicts arise, or when you encounter challenges. Think critically about those responses. Select actions that reflect your fundamental beliefs and professional aspirations rather than simply falling back on familiar habits.

To activate your upgraded internal OS, you need to become an active architect of your character. Don't just be a passenger in your own career story.

How Your Professional Character Changes

Your character isn't set in stone—it's more like a complex database that's been building since childhood. Your earliest "entries" were installed by your primary caregivers. They demonstrated how to act, pointed out where you went wrong, and provided examples—some beneficial for your future, while others could lead you astray.

As time went on, teachers, mentors, coworkers, social media, company cultures, and work experiences brought in fresh viewpoints. Some supported your original programming, while others questioned or went against it. The influences stack up like layers, continually reshaping who you are inside. Some strengthen existing habits, while others create internal conflict and complexity.

Here's the key insight: character becomes habitual, but it's not permanent. You start running on instinct rather than reflection. You deal with stress, navigate success and failure, connect with coworkers, and make career choices based on ingrained habits. These automatic behaviors often feel like part of your identity, but they're not set in stone. They're learned—which means they can be unlearned.

A character reboot starts with examining your current system. You'll identify traits that no longer serve your career goals. Some defaults need to be deleted entirely. Others require significant upgrades. You will need to build some qualities from scratch.

You are the architect of your internal world. You have to choose which qualities to keep, which to rewrite, and which to eliminate. This process requires courage, self-awareness, and clear intention. Most importantly, it demands wisdom—you're rebuilding a system that supports reaching your highest professional and personal potential.

The Science Behind Your Transformation

Modern neuroscience proves what career coaches have long suspected: meaningful change is possible. This occurs due to neuroplasticity, which is your brain's inherent ability to form new neural connections throughout life.

When you opt for a new way to respond professionally, such as remaining calm in stressful situations rather than becoming defensive. Or you choose being dependable instead of frequently being late. You're not just altering your actions, you are changing the way your brain works. When we repeatedly use specific neural pathways, they become stronger. When old patterns are not reinforced, they begin to lose their strength and eventually fade away.

This biological process shows how a character develops over time—not only in theory but also in a tangible way. Change isn't just possible; it's inevitable when you consistently apply the correct principles. The question isn't *whether you can* change your professional character. Neuroscience confirms you can. The real question is, will you take control of that change or let it happen without conscious design or intentionality?

Your Unique Professional Journey

Starting a Character Reboot is deeply personal—it leads to intentional, measurable transformation in your career. Please keep in mind that this journey is unique to you. No two professionals start at the same point, and they won't reach the same destination. That's exactly how it should be.

Your specific combination of strengths and weaknesses, your background, company culture, life experiences, and even your natural temperament all shape where you're starting from. Some professionals are naturally optimistic—they see opportunities everywhere. Other people need to put in more effort to nurture hope and resilience. Some individuals possess a natural aptitude for organization and systematic thinking. Some people find it advantageous to create structure by establishing intentional systems and routines. Be truthful about where you currently stand. Being aware of ourselves is the first step towards making fundamental changes in our lives.

Change impacts individuals in various ways. Some people take to it naturally, viewing it as thrilling, an opportunity to uncover new possibilities and venture into unknown areas. Some people see change as something that can disrupt their lives or even feel like a threat. For them, transformation brings discomfort and a sense of losing control.

The most effective approach honors your natural tendencies rather than fighting against them. If you find yourself resisting change, take a moment to pause and reflect on what's going on. Take a moment to stop and organize your thoughts. Concentrate on building a sense of safety and stability as you grow and change. If you're naturally adaptable, resist the urge to rush through transformation. Instead, be intentional and methodical. Let new patterns take root organically.

Your career goals will determine the outcome of this transformation. What do you want your professional character to reflect? How much effort are you willing to invest in becoming that person?

This is your opportunity. Look inward. Get brutally honest. Define the values you want to live by in your career. Because when your goals become clear, your scattered traits begin to align—and your character becomes a true reflection of your most authentic, successful self.

The Ten Keys to Character Transformation Success

Key #1: Permit Yourself to Change

This isn't about getting a new wardrobe or updating your LinkedIn photo. This is a profound, internal transformation—a fundamental upgrade to who you are as a professional. And it starts with a powerful truth: you are entitled to change.

Yes, you can rewrite, replace, or release traits you've carried for years. Yes, it's not only allowed—it's necessary for your career growth.

Many professionals stumble here. They assume wanting to change means they're fundamentally flawed. They feel guilty about being dissatisfied with their current performance. They worry that evolving somehow betrays their professional history or disappoints others.

That belief isn't simply wrong—it's career-limiting. It keeps talented people trapped in patterns that no longer serve their goals.

The truth? Wanting to grow doesn't mean you're broken. It means you believe in your potential. It means you care enough about your career to stretch beyond your current limits. Allowing yourself to evolve isn't about rejecting your past—it's about investing in your future.

Some family members, friends, or colleagues might prefer you stay the same because it makes them comfortable. Your growth might prompt them to reevaluate their careers—and not everyone is ready for that introspection. But you are. So, permit yourself. Say yes to your professional reboot!

Key #2: Fully Dedicate Yourself

You must make a clear, conscious decision to commit fully to any meaningful Character Reboot. Making a half-hearted effort will not suffice. For real results, you need genuine commitment. This is when you move beyond wishing and into action.

Professional transformation requires active participation. It requires concentrated energy, ongoing effort, and intentional decisions. "Give it your best shot" means putting in all your effort, focus, and bravery into this journey. No matter what challenges you face right now, strive to put forth your best effort—each day, with every choice you make.

This involves setting aside time for genuine self-reflection. It consists of building systems and support structures that will help maintain the changes you aim to achieve. It consists of dedicating your time and energy to books, coaching, mentorship, or other resources that can help you grow. If you're serious about transforming your professional identity, make this a priority over distractions or superficial goals.

Be completely honest with yourself. Where are you right now in your career? Share what might be hindering your progress. Could you identify any patterns that might be hindering you? This is not the time to assign blame or offer justifications. This is a crucial time for self-discovery. It requires bravery to face yourself and recognize what needs to be different, but being truthful is what truly leads to meaningful change.

Take responsibility for your current situation. Take charge of your habits. Take control of your growth. Only you can do this work and create the results you want.

Key #3: Be Prepared for Both Progress and Challenges

Beginning a Character Reboot involves taking a good look at your current thoughts, actions, and attitudes, and then releasing what doesn't help you reach your career aspirations. As you navigate this journey, you can expect to face both surprising breakthroughs and tough roadblocks along the way.

Surprises can drive us to act. You could discover strengths within yourself that you never realized were there. You may have deeper leadership skills than you think. You may find that your skills in strategic thinking and relationship-building are more robust than you realized. These findings can drive your change and enhance your self-assurance.

But frustration is equally inevitable. You'll catch yourself falling back into old patterns. You'll make the same mistake twice or more times. You'll feel like progress is slower than expected. Some days, you'll question whether change is even possible. These are standard and expected reactions.

Successful professionals recognize that both experiences are entirely normal. Discoveries show that change is possible and inspire you to keep moving forward. Challenges reveal where you need to strengthen your approach and help you develop resilience.

It is all about getting your mind ready for both situations—progress and challenges. Take a moment to appreciate your achievements, no matter how minor they may seem. Keep in mind that change takes time; it's a journey, not just one moment. Every professional who has undergone significant character changes has experienced this journey of highs and lows.

Key #4: Concentrate on Systems, Not Only Goals

Having clear career goals is essential, but real and lasting change in character comes from creating better systems. Goals show you what you aim to accomplish, while systems shape your daily actions and future progress.

Rather than simply stating, "I want to be more reliable," try building a system: utilize a task management app, set calendar reminders, and implement a weekly review process. Instead of hoping to "communicate better," build practices: prepare talking points before meetings, practice active listening techniques, and schedule regular check-ins with your team.

Systems enable character change to be automatic rather than dependent on daily motivation. Once you integrate your new habits into your daily routine, maintaining them becomes easier. Lasting professional transformation occurs through steady, organized practice, rather than occasional bursts of effort.

Key #5: Assess Your Growth Clearly

Character change might seem like a vague concept, but when it comes to your professional growth, it is essential to have clear ways to measure it. Focus on tracking specific behaviors instead of just waiting for a change in your feelings.

Create a simple scorecard. To improve your punctuality, keep a record of how often you arrive at meetings on time. As you work on improving your listening skills, pay attention to how you usually ask follow-up questions or restate what others have said. To boost your confidence, record how frequently you share your thoughts in meetings or take on complicated projects.

Weekly reviews are more effective than daily obsessing. Consider trends over time rather than judging individual incidents. Are you improving compared to last month? Which particular behaviors are becoming stronger? What areas do you think you still need to improve in?

This method, based on data, helps you track your progress accurately and allows you to adjust your strategy as needed. It also shows clear proof of your progress, which can help keep your spirits up when times get tough.

Key #6: Uncover What Energizes Your Transformation

Every professional faces moments that reveal their less desirable habits. It is natural to feel a bit on edge about performance reviews. Maybe you find yourself getting frustrated during budget talks. At times, you may procrastinate when handling complex projects.

Recognizing what triggers your emotions is essential for personal growth. When you identify the situations that trigger your old habits, you can prepare new reactions ahead of time. This concept is known as "implementation intentions," which refers to having set plans in place for specific situations.

Develop if-then strategies: "When I sense criticism in a meeting, I'll pause to take three deep breaths and follow up with a question to clarify." "Whenever I begin to feel swamped by a project, I pause for a moment and divide it into three smaller tasks before I continue." "Whenever I feel the need to jump in while someone is talking, I jot down my thought and wait until they finish."

This preparation changes challenging situations from instinctive responses into chances for thoughtful decisions. As time passes, your new responses begin to feel just as natural as the old ones.

Key #7: Establish Your Support System

Transforming a character can be challenging, and attempting to do it alone can make the process even harder. Successful professionals establish support networks that foster their growth and hold them accountable for their progress.

This could involve having a mentor who exemplifies the character traits you wish to cultivate. Furthermore, a group of friends who discuss career growth, along with a coach, can help you identify your blind spots and keep you focused on achieving your goals. Additionally, family members who understand your goals can provide valuable support throughout your journey.

Select supporters who will be truthful with you—not only uplifting but also ready to highlight when you start to revert to previous habits. Allow them the freedom to question you. Share your specific goals with them so they can better understand how to assist you.

Keep in mind that seeking help is not a sign of weakness—it is a smart move. Throughout history, the most successful professionals have always had supporters who believed in them and encouraged their commitment to personal growth.

Key #8: Engage in Practice During Low-Stakes Scenarios

It is not a good idea to try out your new character traits for the first time when you are in the middle of an important presentation or a tough negotiation. Try out your new behaviors in less stressful situations before moving on to the more challenging ones. Work on your patience by using it in everyday chats before trying it out in more intense conversations. As you work on becoming more assertive, begin by practicing in your daily discussions before trying it out in meetings with your superiors. To strengthen your organizational skills, start by refining your system with smaller projects before moving on to bigger tasks.

This method slowly develops both confidence and abilities over time. When you encounter challenging situations, your new reactions come easily, rather than feeling like a battle. You have navigated through the awkward moments and uncertainty in more comfortable settings.

It is similar to acquiring any new skill; you start by practicing the basics, such as scales before a concert, or mastering fundamental techniques before diving into more complex moves. The process of character development works on a similar principle.

Key #9: Embrace Your Journey of Learning

Successful professionals view character development as a continuous journey of learning rather than a quick fix. They often wonder about their actions and are open to feedback.

When things do not go as planned, rather than becoming defensive, they inquire, "What can I take away from this experience?" "What are some other ways I could approach this in the future?" "What pattern do I keep seeing here?"

This mindset transforms mistakes from failures into data. Each interaction is an opportunity to develop the character traits you're cultivating. Every challenging situation becomes an opportunity to try out new ideas.

Explore books that focus on the particular qualities on which you are working. Use the QR code at the end of this book to secure the Companion Workbook to guide your implementation of the OS Reboot. Consider Dr.

A's Character OS Reboot Course if you need major character rehabilitation beyond the scope of this book and the workbook. Check out podcasts featuring experts who represent the traits you aspire to have. Participate in workshops or seminars that focus on character development and growth. Keep yourself involved in the learning process instead of thinking you have got it all figured out.

Key #10: Celebrate Your Transformation

Character change takes work, and it's easy to become discouraged by focusing only on how far you still have to go. Make sure you acknowledge and celebrate the progress you're making along the way.

Note your wins—when you reacted differently than before. Moments when coworkers observed improvements in how you responded to stress. Times when your personal growth led to more successful work experiences. Keep your support network updated on how you are doing. Invite them to join in your celebration. This support strengthens your new habits and encourages ongoing development.

Keep in mind that your goal is not to achieve perfection—it is about being more purposeful in your actions. Every step you take toward becoming the professional you aspire to be is worthy of acknowledgment. This kind of encouragement makes the journey of change more enjoyable and lasting.

Your Character Is Your Career Advantage

The professionals who thrive in today's competitive environment aren't necessarily the smartest or most skilled. They're the ones who have developed strong character foundations that support consistent peak performance. They've moved beyond technical competence to master the internal operating system that drives all their external results.

Your character is what sets you apart from the competition. Your career success depends more on your Character Database than your LLM. In a world where everyone has access to the same information and similar training, what truly makes you unique is your character. It's about how you handle stress, work with others, make decisions, and put in daily effort.

Ambitious professionals utilize the ten keys we've discussed as practical tools to empower their careers. When you upgrade your character operating system, everything else begins to improve: your relationships, reputation, results, and opportunities.

You have everything you need to begin this transformation today. The question isn't whether you're capable of change—neuroscience proves you are. The question is whether you're ready to take control of that change and direct it toward the professional future you want. Your career is waiting for the upgraded version of you. The only question left is when you will start.

Anonymous

"Many people would be scared if they saw in the mirror not their faces but their character."

CHAPTER 5

The Four Pillars of Character: Your Developmental Blueprint

Zig Ziglar

"It was character that got us out of bed, commitment that moved us into action, and discipline that enabled us to follow through."

The Architecture of Character

Designing Your Professional Identity

You have likely tried the conventional fixes. You've perused productivity books, experimented with the newest project management applications, engaged in extensive networking, and perhaps even refined your resume numerous times. But none of it has addressed the core issue. Why? Your resume, skills, or strategy are not the bottleneck. It's not external. The problem, and therefore the solution, lies within. It's your internal operating system—your character.

Think about the operating system (OS) on your phone or computer. When it's new and running smoothly, it's invisible, and everything works exactly right. However, as new demands arise and technology continues to evolve, the same OS can become buggy, slow, and insecure over time. Apps start crashing, simple tasks take forever, and the entire system becomes a source of frustration. You wouldn't blame the apps; you'd know the underlying OS needs a fundamental update.

Your character is the personal OS of your professional life. It's the complex, invisible code running in the background of every interaction, decision, and challenge you face. It's the source code for your discipline, your integrity, your resilience, and your ability to connect with others. When your Character OS is outdated, it develops "bugs"—like a tendency to avoid difficult conversations, a fear of taking risks, or a habit of micromanaging your team. This leads to a sense of immobility. It's the professional equivalent of the spinning wheel of death, and no surface-level "hack" can fix it.

The fantastic news is that, unlike your personality, which is relatively stable, your character is malleable. Just like a tech OS, it can be debugged, upgraded, and optimized for high performance. This chapter provides the detailed blueprint for that reboot. It's a practical, evidence-informed framework built on four pillars that will guide you from vague awareness to deliberate action. This is your path to turning your core values into the consistent, daily behaviors that deliver results, rebuild your credibility, and reignite your career trajectory.

The Four Pillars of Character

When an architect starts designing a skyscraper, they don't begin by choosing curtains for the penthouse. They start with the basics: the structural steel and the core support systems—these are the key components that ensure the building can withstand tremendous pressure and remain standing strong for a hundred years. Building a powerful professional identity requires the same architectural rigor. You need a blueprint.

This framework breaks down the complex concept of character into four clear, distinct, and manageable pillars. These ideas are not merely theoretical; they serve as the essential building blocks for a successful and rewarding career. They offer a straightforward method to identify your weaknesses and purposefully enhance your strengths. To make them tangible and easy to remember, each pillar is connected to a vital natural element, grounding these principles in the real world.

- **Being:** The pure, life-sustaining water of your core identity.
- **Feeling:** The vital, invisible oxygen of your relationships and emotional intelligence.
- **Doing:** The tangible, impactful atmosphere of your public life and professional execution.
- **Becoming:** The lively and forward-thinking energy of your growth and the opportunities that lie ahead.

In the following chapters, we will take a closer look at each of these pillars. It is essential to understand that character is not just a random mix of positive traits. It's a system where each part works together. They all influence one another. This creates a strong and unified whole. If one area is weak, it can manifest itself in other areas.

Assets and Liabilities

The Balance Sheet of Your Character

Before you begin building, it is vital to take a transparent and honest look at the materials you have on hand. Imagine your character as a financial balance sheet, showcasing both the assets that generate value and the liabilities that introduce risk.

- A **character asset** is a valuable skill that enhances your professional reputation. Having traits such as integrity, discipline, empathy, and accountability helps build trust, improve teamwork, and enable you to provide reliable value.

These are the foundations of a solid reputation. This reboot program identifies forty character assets that enhance your life.

- A **character liability** is a flaw that quietly undermines your advancement. Habits such as dishonesty, laziness, arrogance, or shifting blame can undermine trust, hurt relationships, and weaken your professional impact. These are the concealed liabilities that can ruin a career. This reboot identifies forty character liabilities that impair your life.

The Character Reboot process involves taking a closer look at oneself. It's about taking a clear-eyed, courageous look at your ledger to identify your liabilities, transform them into assets, and sharpen the assets you already possess. This is not about being overly critical of ourselves or striving for something impossible to achieve. It's about applying compassionate self-awareness to see yourself more clearly.

Understanding your personal balance sheet—and how your liabilities can flip into assets—is the foundational first step. It allows you to build a character that actively supports your career goals, rather than silently and mysteriously undermining them.

Why This Matters in Your Professional Life

Understanding this developmental framework clarifies why even top professionals may face character-related challenges. A successful executive might struggle with personal relationships, indicating a need to improve in the Feeling pillar. A capable manager might struggle to follow through, revealing weaknesses in the Doing pillar. A high achiever may feel stuck or unsatisfied, indicating a weak pillar of the Becoming.

This reboot process names your development areas and reinforces your strengths. It highlights recurring patterns and offers a structured, strategic approach—much more effective than random trial and error.

The Developmental Journey: How Character Matures

The Four Pillars—Being, Feeling, Doing, and Becoming—are intentionally arranged. They stand for a natural progression of human growth and increasing impact.

1. **Being comes first.** It strengthens your self-relationship. During early childhood, you start to develop your identity, confidence, and core values. The core elements show the foundation of your character.

2. **Feeling comes after.** It helps you build stronger connections with your family, friends, and professional colleagues. Emotional intelligence is about recognizing and managing your emotions. It also means grasping how other people are feeling. Maintaining healthy relationships and collaborating effectively are essential.

3. **Next up is Doing.** The choices you make in school, sports, or work show how involved you are with the world around you. Your reliability and sense of responsibility make people trust you, showing what kind of person you are.

4. **Becoming is the last step.** It broadens your perspective from your current activities to your future growth, lasting effects, and valuable contributions. Your identity and purpose are constantly evolving and impacting your life.

Introducing the Four Character Pillars

Let us further explore the Four Pillars of Character, each of which is connected to an essential aspect of life. These analogies connect abstract ideas to their real-world importance. They demonstrate how these ideas contribute to the development of a comprehensive professional identity.

The Being Pillar: The Water of Your Character

Water is essential for life. It plays a key role in our bodies and is a big part of who we are. Your Being pillar acts as the foundation of who you are. It governs your relationship with yourself—your core values, self-awareness, integrity, and inner sense of worth. This pillar is about authenticity. Your internal compass ensures that your external actions align with your deepest beliefs, even when no one is observing.

A Being pillar means you are anchored. External validation or criticism doesn't easily shake your quiet confidence. You act with integrity even when it's the harder choice. A weak Being pillar, however, leaves you adrift. This manifests as a weak sense of self. This makes you more likely to feel like an imposter. You might constantly seek approval from others. You could also make ethical compromises when under pressure. Even when you reach your goals, you might still feel empty inside.

Real-World Example: Julia

Julia was an accomplished project manager. She portrayed complete control and competence. She secretly feared failure. A spotless record was crucial to her self-esteem. Her staff identified a significant data issue as a client deadline approached. Her feeble support system was activated. She was terrified of making a mistake and ruining her perfect image. Instead of admitting the mistake, she asked her team to work around it to avoid detection.

The client review uncovered the cover-up, and the effects were rapid and devastating. Deception, not error, was the cause of the damage. Her credibility was lost in an instant, and years of trust were broken. A tough public failure was her unwanted turning point. Without her carefully formed facade, she faced her frailty. She began the complicated process of character restoration through coaching. Radical honesty was her top value, and she started her relaunch by apologizing to her team and client and taking full responsibility. In the ensuing year, she focused on her Being pillar, honesty, confidence, and self-worth based on ideals rather than performance. She acquired more respect and resilience from this new basis of integrity than from her former image of perfection.

The Feeling Pillar: The Oxygen of Your Character

Oxygen is the unseen, essential part of living that keeps us alive. It powers every cell in our body, allowing us to have energy, function properly, and live active lives. Your Feeling pillar is like the vital "oxygen" in your career—it's the unseen force that drives your connections, teamwork, and support. This pillar represents your emotional intelligence (EI), which is crucial for recognizing and managing your own emotions, as well as understanding, empathizing with, and influencing the feelings of others.

You can be the best in the organization, but if your Feeling pillar is weak, you'll stall. Team morale will plummet, collaboration will break down, good people will leave, and others will brush aside your attempts at leadership. If you've ever thought, "I'm technically proficient, but I just can't seem to rally my team," or "People seem to misinterpret my intentions," a weakness in this pillar is almost certainly the cause. This is a significant cause of professional demise.

Real-World Example: David

David was a department head recognized for his sharp intelligence and impatience. He was aggressive in meetings but also an effective strategist. He would interrupt people mid-sentence, publicly reject negative ideas, and sigh and roll his eyes in frustration. His actions poisoned creativity and psychological safety. His teammates became mute, feeling their contributions were undesired and their ideas meaningless. Fear of being shot down prevented great ideas from being shared. Department turnover was the highest in the company.

The reboot began when his supervisor told him the truth after a performance review: "David, your outcomes are excellent, but your wake is terrible. You are an unfollowable leader." Feedback shook his system, and he concentrated on his Feeling pillar in a character reboot. His painful first practice was to listen more than he spoke in every conversation. Instead of assuming, he forced himself to ask, "Tell me more about that." Despite his disagreements, he publicly acknowledged and validated others' contributions ("Thanks, Sarah, I appreciate you bringing that perspective"). The mood changed slowly and painfully. People spoke up again. The energy of the meeting shifted from fear to active involvement. David understood that authentic leadership was about making everyone wiser and more courageous, not just being brilliant.

The Doing Pillar: The Atmosphere of Your Character

The Earth's atmosphere acts like a shield. It protects us from harmful things in space. It controls temperature and burns up meteorites. It creates the pressure needed for life to exist. This layer is real and valuable and helps our world function. Your Doing pillar is the "atmosphere" that protects your professional reputation. It's all about your actions in the world—your reliability, your discipline, your accountability, and the quality of your follow-through. This is the foundation where your aspirations and promises become tangible results. It is all about how your commitments align with your accomplishments.

A strong Doing pillar builds a reliable shield of trust that envelops you. When people see you as reliable—someone who meets deadlines, keeps promises, and does excellent work—they are more likely to assign you bigger responsibilities. This is the way careers are developed. A weak Doing pillar, on the other hand, makes you open and susceptible. It gives you a reputation for being untrustworthy, someone who talks excessively, and does not produce. This results in shattered trust, average performance, and a career that feels like it is going nowhere.

Real-World Example: Elenor

Elenor's tech startup was on the verge of collapse. A vital funding round had failed; her co-founder had departed. A key supplier had gone bankrupt, causing supply chain upheaval—a perfect storm of failure. While under pressure, many leaders would have panicked or blamed others. However, Elenor's mighty Doing pillar accelerated. Her character became the company's most important asset.

Instead of suppressing terrible news, she brutally informed her small, terrified workforce about the situation. She then put together a detailed 30-day survival plan that focused on the most critical tasks. She worked tirelessly, consistently arriving first and leaving last, and personally handled the most challenging calls with irate suppliers and worried clients. In the midst of pandemonium, her meticulous execution and uncompromising accountability brought steadiness. Her teammates were devoted to her because of her perseverance. A new investor was more impressed by her crisis leadership than by her company concept due to her reliability and follow-through. The company survived and thrived. Elenor became known not just for having a grand vision but for being a leader who reliably achieved results, no matter what obstacles came her way.

The Becoming Pillar: The Energy of Your Character

Energy is the essential force that powers all movement, change, and transformation throughout the universe. It's lively and progressive, working against the natural drift toward disorder and decline. Your Becoming pillar is the driving force that pushes your career ahead. Your wisdom, creativity, generosity, and flexibility are your strengths. This is the pillar that saves you from becoming professionally obsolete in a world of constant change.

A solid Becoming pillar supports a growth mindset. It motivates you to acquire new skills, pursue fresh challenges, and adjust to changing technologies and market needs. It's what enables you to transform yourself throughout a lengthy career. A weak Becoming pillar, on the other hand, results in stagnation. It reveals a reluctance to embrace change and a tendency to cling to traditional methods ("this is how we have always done it"). There is a disinterest in exploring what lies ahead, and it is the gradual decline to irrelevance.

Real-World Example: James

James gained a lot of respect as a senior executive. He possesses a wealth of knowledge and extensive experience, particularly in his late 50s. He had reached the top of his career. He could have looked forward to a relaxing retirement. Yet, he began to feel increasingly out of place as artificial intelligence transformed his field. The other senior executives either ignored AI or were afraid of it. James intentionally activated his Becoming pillar at this crucial moment.

He took an online executive AI course. More crucially, he held "reverse mentoring" sessions with junior data scientists in his organization, saying, "I know our business, but you know this new world. I need your instruction." This humility and openness to learn energized his staff. He led a pilot effort to optimize a business process with AI. The project's success made him a forward-thinking leader, not a relic of the past. This proactive relaunch revitalized his work over the last decade. It fostered a culture of continuous learning within his division, demonstrating that significant growth can occur at any time if you are dedicated to personal development.

The Interconnected Nature of Character Elements

The Four Pillars are not four separate projects; they are a single, integrated system, like the four cylinders in an engine. For peak performance, all four must be firing correctly. If one pillar is weak, it will eventually bring down the others, slowing down your whole career. This is why attempting to correct just one isolated behavior usually doesn't work—it overlooks the underlying interconnected cause.

Take a look at this typical professional profile: A manager truly shines in the Doing pillar. He works really well, stays organized, and always gets his work done on time. However, Feeling pillar is not fully developed. He frequently displays impatience, has difficulty listening, and rarely provides compliments. As a result, his team feels disconnected and underperforms. His results ultimately suffer from their lackluster performance, which portrays him as a "great individual contributor, but not a leader." He cannot just "do" his way out of a "feeling" issue.

Growth happens in a natural order, moving through the stages of Being → Feeling → Doing → Becoming.

Building genuine and reliable relationships with others begins with having a solid understanding of who you are and what you stand for (Being). Creating solid connections is essential for effective collaboration and achieving success (Feeling). Consistent, high-quality execution (Doing) helps establish the credibility and momentum necessary for achieving growth. The icing on the cake is the vision and energy to forge an unknown future with dispatch and acumen (Becoming). Grasping this sequence serves as an effective diagnostic tool. It allows you to trace the origins of your career obstacles. If you're having a hard time getting things done, the issue might not be your productivity methods; it could be the fragile connections with your team, which often arise from a lack of confidence or self-awareness. This framework allows you to go beyond merely handling symptoms and start addressing the root problems in a considerate manner.

Transforming Awareness into Action

Recognizing the Four Pillars is just the first step. To make this insight lead to real change, it is vital to have a straightforward way to evaluate your current character profile, identifying both your natural strengths and areas where you can grow. Insight alone is insufficient. Practical tools are essential to guide and support that transformation. Chapters 10 and 11 address these issues. These chapters elaborate on the key tools for your character reboot, now and in the future:

- **Character Database** is where your character priorities reside. It is here where critical review and assessment take place. It is the control center for current and future development.
- **Character Praxis-Loop** is what pushes you to grow. This is where we apply what we have learned in theory to real-world situations. Your daily habits, decisions, conversations, and mindset shifts reflect your evolving character deliberately and consistently.
- The Character **OS Tune-Up Manual** is what keeps your high-performance character in tip-top shape. Without a maintenance program, our best intentions can slowly fade or erode. Regular tending to the character soil keeps the fruits healthy and alive.

The Path Forward

The following four chapters (six to nine) will provide a detailed examination of the Four Pillars in a professional setting—Being, Feeling, Doing, and Becoming. I will offer practical insights and strategies to enhance your strengths and manage your weaknesses.

Your essence (Being), which is like water, influences how you see yourself and your inner direction. This, in turn, helps you feel more connected to other people emotionally (Feeling). Your actions (Doing) contribute to the atmosphere you create, which ultimately shapes your reputation. Your energy (Becoming) empowers all of this, driving your growth, vision, and long-term impact. The Four Pillars establish a comprehensive framework for developing character that extends beyond merely adhering to a basic list of dos and don'ts. They are not distinct compartments but rather coordinated forces.

The aim is not perfection. The main goal is to make progress. The objective is to boost your professional presence by being more deliberate, authentic, and impactful. Your body requires all vital systems to work together, and similarly, your character needs balance across all four pillars to achieve its full potential.

Your aim is not to turn yourself into someone else; it is to be the best version of yourself. The Four Pillars provide a comprehensive foundation for this change, and the strategies in the following chapters lay out the practical steps to make it happen. By establishing a solid framework and demonstrating commitment, you can cultivate a character that propels you toward professional success, personal satisfaction, and meaningful impact. The internal water, oxygen, atmosphere, and energy are fundamental elements for your character transformation.

In the chapters ahead, we will take a closer look at each of these pillars. You will examine the key strengths that enhance each area and identify the weaknesses that could undermine them. You will acquire the clarity and knowledge needed to embark on a crucial personal project: developing character content that serves as your key professional asset and the foundation for a rewarding future.

Dr. A's Character Chart can be found at the end of this chapter.

Dr. A's Character Chart is a useful visual tool that displays the whole four-pillar framework. It outlines character development in four straightforward levels: Being, Feeling, Doing, and Becoming, and organizes eighty specific traits into these categories. This chart illustrates the entire journey of human character development, beginning with self-awareness (Being) and leading to lifelong leadership (Becoming). Each pillar has twenty contrasting characteristics. Ten assets that enhance your confidence, encourage achievement, and foster trust. Ten liabilities that hinder your progress, deter achievement, and foster a lack of trust. Dr. A's Character Chart enables you to assess your strengths and weaknesses visually, offering a clearer insight into your current self and the areas that need attention.

The Three Roles of the Character Chart

1. A Comprehensive View of Character Complexity

Dr. A's chart showcases character traits within a distinctive, integrated framework. It acknowledges the complexity and diversity of human behavior. No one will possess all 80 characteristics since some are mutually exclusive and potentially conflicting with one another.

A compassionate individual is unlikely to hold deep resentment. A careless individual often misses the details that a responsible individual notices. Respect and tact are interconnected, contrasting with selfishness and intolerance. Without humility, confidence can quickly turn into arrogance.

2. A Global Mirror for Self-Evaluation

This chart serves as a self-assessment tool. Do you have more liabilities than assets? Do your eyes focus more on the top than the bottom or vice versa? What traits stand out to you and are most prominent in your current character operating system? What traits do you want to develop or change?

The top forty assets will enhance your character, promote your career, and help you achieve your goals. The forty liabilities listed below will hinder progress and reduce your influence. Identify the obstacles holding you back and begin the intentional process of transforming them into strengths. In two words, move upwards!

3. Progressive Character Development Paradigm

The Character Chart shows how traits develop and evolve throughout your story. This illustrates how your character has evolved from left to right, emphasizing the growth of your influence over time.

To build effectively, begin on the left side of the chart and move to the right, concentrating on each pillar one at a time. Building up your internal strengths—your core assets—creates a solid base for significant growth in every other area. When you work on improving one pillar of your life, it can also help enhance the other pillars of your life. This will have a significant, positive effect on both your life and your career.

In Conclusion

Examining your character can sometimes be uncomfortable. You might come across habits, attitudes, or patterns that are no longer serving you. It can be challenging to see that you lack the basic assets or that character liabilities are stunting your growth. These blind spots could be causing some problems in your relationships, how you handle your emotions, or even your career progression.

Your current situation does not decide your future. Your limitations right now don't define who you are. You are empowered to make a difference. Real change begins with one choice: to grow. Keep a positive mindset. Try not to get caught up in the idea of being perfect. Make sure to focus on your progress by being intentional, being true to yourself, and leading with a clear purpose. The things you do and what you believe in will shape who you turn out to be.

Key Takeaways

1. Your character functions as your operating system. It influences how you think, feel, act, and grow—and it can be intentionally improved.

2. The Four Pillars framework maps your growth path. Four interconnected elements form the foundation of a thriving professional life: Being (Water), Feeling (Oxygen), Doing (Atmosphere), and Becoming (Energy).

3. Every trait has potential—but also risk. If you do not nourish your strengths, they may degrade into weaknesses. Weaknesses can turn into strengths if you focus on them. For a character to grow sustainably, they need to attain a healthy balance, with the asset being the dominant one or replacing the liability.

4. Growth happens in a natural order. First, you are → then you feel → next, you do → and finally, you become. Every pillar supports the one before it, illustrating how individuals grow and evolve.

5. The pillars rely on each other. If any pillar is deficient, it can compromise the entire system. This highlights the importance of self-assessment, particularly for individuals seeking to grow and restart a stalled career.

Stephen Covey

"Just as we strengthen our physical muscles by overcoming opposition, such as lifting weights, we develop our character by overcoming challenges and adversity."

Character Chart

 ## Dr. A's Character Makeover Chart
Character Assets and Character Liabilities

Assets

Being	Feeling	Doing	Becoming
Character assets which **enhances** living with yourself!	Character assets which **enhances** relating to family!	Character assets which **enhances** your public life!	Character assets which **enhances** your future!
☐ 1. Alive	☐ 11. Attentive	☐ 21. Accountable	☐ 31. Courageous
☐ 2. Confident	☐ 12. Authentic	☐ 22. Deferential	☐ 32. Creative
☐ 3. Conscientious	☐ 13. Empathetic	☐ 23. Dependable	☐ 33. Adaptable
☐ 4. Decisive	☐ 14. Forgiving	☐ 24. Diligent	☐ 34. Focused
☐ 5. Disciplined	☐ 15. Grateful	☐ 25. Organized	☐ 35. Generous
☐ 6. Honest	☐ 16. Loyal	☐ 26. Punctual	☐ 36. Just
☐ 7. Honorable	☐ 17. Patient	☐ 27. Responsible	☐ 37. Optimistic
☐ 8. Humble	☐ 18. Respectful	☐ 28. Tactful	☐ 38. Persuasive
☐ 9. Caring	☐ 19. Sociable	☐ 29. Thorough	☐ 39. Prudent
☐ 10. Passionate	☐ 20. Trusting	☐ 30. Tolerant	☐ 40. Wise

> "Whether everyone is watching, or no one is watching, I owe it to myself <u>to be</u>, <u>to feel</u>, <u>to do</u> and <u>to become</u> my very best self."

Liabilities

Being	Feeling	Doing	Becoming
Character liabilities which **impairs** living with yourself!	Character liabilities which **impairs** relating to family!	Character liabilities which **impairs** your public life!	Character liabilities which **impairs** your future!
☐ 41. Lifeless	☐ 51. Inattentive	☐ 61. Unreliable	☐ 71. Fainthearted
☐ 42. Diffident	☐ 52. Phony	☐ 62. Arrogant	☐ 72. Unimaginative
☐ 43. Unprincipled	☐ 53. Apathetic	☐ 63. Undependable	☐ 73. Inflexible
☐ 44. Indecisive	☐ 54. Resentful	☐ 64. Lazy	☐ 74. Procrastinate
☐ 45. Undisciplined	☐ 55. Complaintive	☐ 65. Disorganized	☐ 75. Greedy
☐ 46. Deceitful	☐ 56. Disloyal	☐ 66. Tardy	☐ 76. Unjust
☐ 47. Callous	☐ 57. Impatient	☐ 67. Irresponsible	☐ 77. Pessimistic
☐ 48. Conceited	☐ 58. Rude	☐ 68. Reckless	☐ 78. Dissuasive
☐ 49. Uncaring	☐ 59. Unsociable	☐ 69. Sloppy	☐ 79. Wasteful
☐ 50. Unmotivated	☐ 60. Jealous	☐ 70. Intolerant	☐ 80. Foolish

©2019 Dr. A's Character

CHAPTER 6

The "Being" Pillar: Clean, Life-Sustaining Water

Ernest Hemingway

"Character is grace under pressure."

Welcome to the heart of the machine, the core of your Character OS. This chapter can help you start over if your career is stagnant. You may have attempted various strategies. These include productivity tips, networking methods, and skills courses. Yet, you still feel stagnant in your job. Meanwhile, others progress, making you feel overlooked and undervalued.

The main issue lies within us, not outside, so those outside strategies have failed. It is part of your "Being" pillar. This pillar is your internal Kernel, the strong code that operates behind every action you take. It governs your professional identity, your gut intuition, and your inner alignment. It's composed of fundamental traits like confidence, discipline, and integrity. These very qualities determine how you perceive yourself long before you ever step into a meeting or send an email. Your caregivers and early experiences may have written the first version of this code. Still, as a professional experiencing the immense friction of stagnation, it is now your responsibility to debug and upgrade it.

This is the "inner work" you suspect is necessary. This pillar is the life-sustaining water of your character; without it, every other part of your professional life becomes barren. A deficit here is what creates that invisible ceiling, and strengthening it is how you'll finally shatter it.

TABLE A

"Being" Character Assets (Momentum Builders)	"Being" Character Liabilities (Stagnation Traps)
1. Alive	41. Lifeless
2. Confident	42. Diffident
3. Conscientious	43. Unprincipled
4. Decisive	44. Indecisive
5. Disciplined	45. Undisciplined
6. Honest	46. Deceitful
7. Honorable	47. Callous
8. Humble	48. Conceited
9. Caring	49. Uncaring
10. Passionate	50. Unmotivated

Before delving into these characteristics, pose a challenging question to yourself that reveals the underlying cause of your professional stagnation. When you are alone with your thoughts, what are you saying and thinking to yourself? I am not sure what you are asking. Does your inner voice provide clarity and truth, or does it fill you with doubts that hold you back? Answering honestly is the first step toward the profound career reboot you're seeking. We seek a reset that restores credibility, reignites momentum, and paves the way for the peak performance that has felt so out of reach.

This chapter looks at the Being pillar and the first ten pairs of assets and liabilities. We will define each trait as a practical tool for your career, not just an abstract virtue. We will examine how its presence or absence is affecting your current stagnation or your chances for a breakthrough. The aim is not to be perfect; it is to take intentional, strong steps to shape your progress.

The Foundation Balance Sheet

1. Alive vs. 41. Lifeless

The Liability of Being Lifeless: A lifeless professional is more than just quiet or unmotivated; they are invisible. This employee drains energy from the room. Their main trait is a passive disinterest. This can be easily mistaken for a lack of ability or a lack of commitment. You may notice this in yourself: you complete only the minimum work required and remain quiet in meetings where your input is necessary. You frequently glance at the clock, indicating that you would prefer to be elsewhere. This isn't just introversion; it's a broadcast of disengagement. For the ambitious professional who feels stuck, this is a fatal flaw. Leaders do not promote people who seem to have given up. A lifeless demeanor is a self-fulfilling prophecy of stagnation; it confirms to others that you are not hungry for more. It makes it easy to overlook you for the next big project or promotion. Your lack of vitality is the reason your visibility has faded to zero.

The Asset of Being Alive: In contrast, an alive professional is impossible to ignore. This is not about being forced to be cheerful; it is about showing real energy and genuine passion for the work, as well as a dedication to common goals that drive it. When you are alive, you don't wait for an invitation; you ask thoughtful questions. You cheer for others' successes and see challenges as opportunities to grow. This energy is infectious. It draws in allies, sparks new ideas, and identifies you as a natural leader, regardless of your official title. For someone stuck in their career, developing this trait is the best way to overcome being overlooked. This trait causes decision-makers to perceive you differently, viewing you not merely as someone who complies but as an active contributor capable of handling greater responsibility.

The Growth Path from Lifeless to Alive: To transition from feeling lifeless to alive and get your career moving again, you need to discover what excites you about your work. Begin with small steps and pick a small but intriguing part of your job and offer to lead a project about it. For your next team meeting, bring one thoughtful question that demonstrates you are considering more than just your current tasks. Be sure to recognize a coworker's contribution in front of others. These actions are the antidote to professional inertia. You will shift from being the person who drains energy to the one who creates it, making yourself a catalyst for success and an undeniable candidate for advancement.

2. Confident vs. 42. Diffident

The Liability of Being Diffident: A diffident professional is confined by an invisible barrier they have created for themselves. The root of the problem is this sense of personal immobility. You have the skills and the experience, but self-doubt paralyzes you. You often hesitate to share your best ideas, beginning with phrases like, "I might be asking a silly question, but..." You avoid leadership roles and let others take charge because you are worried about making mistakes. This shyness is not considered a sign of humility; instead, it is perceived as a reflection of low confidence and capability. Your silence during critical times deprives the team of valuable insights and creates uncertainty. Your career has stalled because your diffidence signals to others that you do not believe you are ready for the next level, and as a result, they share that perception.

The Asset of Being Confident: A confident professional is the stabilizing force on any team and the architect of their ascent. This is not arrogance; it is a quiet, steady trust in one's ability to add value and navigate challenges. Confident professionals express their opinions respectfully, even if they disagree. When issues arise, they focus on finding solutions rather than placing blame, which helps build trust with coworkers and clients. They take on complex projects, demonstrating to the entire organization that they can handle challenges. This decisiveness drives progress, pushing the whole team ahead and identifying you as a leader even before you have the title. This is how you change from feeling stuck to being in demand.

The Growth Path from Diffident to Confident: Moving from being diffident to being confident involves creating a collection of evidence to support your confidence. Begin by taking calculated risks in situations with minimal stakes. At your next meeting, consider taking the initiative to share a thoughtful opinion first. Take on a challenging task that stretches your limits, showing yourself and others that you can manage it. Quit saying sorry for your ideas. Express them clearly and confidently. This is not about bragging; it is about quietly recognizing the worth you contribute. Every small act of confidence breaks down that invisible barrier until it finally breaks, opening up the way for the reward you deserve.

3. Conscientious vs. 43. Unprincipled

The Liability of Being Unprincipled: An unprincipled professional may notice their influence diminishing and their network contracting, often without understanding the reasons behind it. This isn't about grand criminal acts; it's about the slow erosion of trust caused by small, self-serving decisions. It's miscrediting a teammate's idea or promising a client something you can't deliver. It's cutting corners on a report or shifting blame when a mistake is yours. These actions, caused by weak Being character, might confer a temporary benefit, but they create a harmful environment and ruin your most important career asset: your reputation. If you feel your career has stalled, it may be because key stakeholders no longer trust you. They won't give you critical tasks or sponsor your promotion if they believe you prioritize your gain over the integrity of the work and the success of the team.

The Asset of Being Conscientious: A conscientious professional is characterized by their strong moral compass, which makes them the most reliable and trusted individual in the room. They are characterized by their responsibility, integrity, and honesty. They work late to verify the data, make shared checklists to avoid mistakes, and are quick to acknowledge errors and suggest solutions. This strong commitment to quality and ethical behavior creates a solid reputation for integrity. Your reputation is valuable for your career. It opens up essential assignments, gains the trust of senior leaders, and ensures your advancement is a reliable choice for the organization. If you are very conscientious, you don't have to struggle for attention; your dependability makes you indispensable.

The Growth Path from Unprincipled to Conscientious: To shift from an unprincipled to a conscientious mindset, you must commit to being 100% reliable and trustworthy. You will assume complete responsibility for your work and always aim to provide the best quality, even when no one is observing. Proactively create systems, like checklists, to prevent errors. If an error occurs, address it promptly and openly. Cease any behavior that puts your gain ahead of the team's success—no more stolen credit, no more blame-shifting. Your goal is to make it an effortless decision for anyone to entrust you with their most important work. This is how you rebuild burned bridges and restore the credibility needed to move your career forward again.

4. Decisive vs. 44. Indecisive

The Liability of Being Indecisive: A person who struggles to make decisions can hinder their team's progress and their own career advancement. This is the person who always needs "just one more piece of data" or changes a decision made in a meeting the next day—this hesitation and self-doubt cause delays and uncertainty for the whole team. No one knows the exact way ahead. If you feel stuck in your role, indecisiveness may be a significant reason. Struggling with the pressure and uncertainty of higher roles demonstrates leadership. Not deciding and sticking to it leaves you in situations where others make choices for you.

The Asset of Being Decisive: A decisive professional creates momentum. They offer the clarity and guidance that teams need, especially when under pressure. When faced with unexpected budget cuts or shifting priorities, they don't waffle. They gather the necessary information, make a sensible judgment, and communicate a clear path forward. "We are cutting Feature X to stay on budget. Here is the revised plan." This reduces confusion and focuses the team's energy. It builds trust and confidence. Decisiveness shows strong leadership. This is true regardless of your title. This demonstrates your ability to manage complexity. It shows you are prepared for increased responsibility.

The Journey from Indecisive to Decisive: To break free from indecision, begin by making choices in smaller situations—give yourself deadlines for your decisions. When you have options, it can be helpful to set a time limit for yourself. Gather the best information you can within the specified timeframe, plan accordingly, and proceed. Get used to making "good enough" decisions instead of waiting for a perfect, risk-free solution that will never come. Making quick, smart decisions on small tasks helps you develop your skills and establish a reputation as someone who gets things done. This changes you from someone who holds things up to a person who drives progress, showing everyone that you are prepared to lead.

5. Disciplined vs. 45. Undisciplined

The Liability of Being Undisciplined: A professional in a career rut may face a silent threat to their credibility if they lack discipline. This isn't about being lazy; it's about being inconsistent. You begin projects with a lot of energy, but lose motivation before completing them. You mention you'll "get back to me with the data" or "write that proposal," but it hasn't happened yet. Your inability to fully trust yourself with essential tasks is evident in your repeated missed deadlines and incomplete tasks. Your career has stalled because your hard work, even if intense, is not yielding the desired results. Leaders and coworkers may begin to doubt your abilities. They might assign important tasks to someone they trust more. Your lack of discipline poses a risk. It hinders your ability to seize opportunities.

The Asset of Being Disciplined: Discipline is essential for success in any career. It is often overlooked. It involves a dedication to executing plans with reliability and consistency. A disciplined professional understands that consistent habits, rather than sporadic efforts, result in excellence. They are the person who consistently shows up, does the work, and keeps their promises. They build systems to maintain quality, manage their energy effectively, and view every promise as a commitment to their reputation. This constant reliability creates a strong sense of trust around you. Being disciplined makes you the person others rely on for essential projects. Your name is known for being completed and completed successfully. Here's how to break the cycle of stagnation. Your actions demonstrate your certainty, making your promotion a matter of when, not if.

The Journey from Undisciplined to Disciplined: To escape being undisciplined, you need to create systems instead of just depending on willpower. Start by making your word your bond. For the next two weeks, do not make a single professional promise—to yourself or others—that you are not 100% certain you can keep. Concentrate your commitments on a select few that you can manage effectively and carry out accurately. Utilize external tools such as calendars, task managers, and checklists. These can help reduce the mental burden of remembering tasks. Your objective is to establish a history of unquestionable dependability. Every promise you keep helps rebuild your reputation. It also restores the momentum lost due to inconsistency and a lack of discipline.

6. Honest vs. 46. Deceitful

The Liability of Being Deceitful: A deceitful professional operates on a foundation of sand, and for the stalled professional, this is a fatal architecture. Deceit in the workplace is rarely about grand conspiracy; it's a series of small, corrosive lies. It's glossing over negative results in a report, blaming a missed deadline on a vague "technical issue" when it was actually poor planning. Or staying silent when you know a project is heading for disaster. You may believe you're managing perceptions, but this approach could be compromising your most valuable asset: your credibility. Eventually, the truth emerges, as it always does. Once your colleagues and leaders see that you manipulate or conceal the truth, they will lose trust in your judgment and reports. Your deceit as a reality narrator stalls your career and jeopardizes the future of your part of the organization.

The Asset of Being Honest: In a professional setting, honesty means being completely and responsibly transparent. A truthful professional understands that early disclosure of adverse news can rectify the situation but withholding it can result in more significant problems later. They readily admit their mistakes and suggest solutions, saying things like, "I made a mistake, and here's how I plan to rectify it," or "My initial projections were incorrect; we need to reevaluate." This is not a weakness; it is an immense strength. It provides the entire organization with the clean, unfiltered data needed to make the best possible decisions. This kind of honesty builds a rare and powerful form of trust. It positions you not just as an implementer, but as a trusted advisor. When you are known as the person who will tell the truth even when it's hard, you are given access to the most critical conversations and decisions—the very arenas where careers are made.

The Journey from Deceitful to Honest: To transform from deceitful (or even truth-averse) to rigorously honest, you must reframe truth-telling as a strategic advantage. For your next project, make a pact with yourself to be the single source of truth for your team. Proactively identify and communicate risks before they become problems. When you make a mistake, report it to your direct supervisor within the hour—not with excuses, but with a clear-eyed assessment and a proposed solution. This will feel uncomfortable at first. But with each act of fearless honesty, you will feel the ground beneath you solidify, rebuilding the trust needed to get your career moving forward with unstoppable momentum.

7. Honorable vs. 47. Callous

The Liability of Being Callous: The callous professional perceives their colleagues as obstacles or tools, rather than recognizing them as individuals. This is a direct output of EgoOS's primary directive to ascend, often at the expense of others. They show little concern for the human impact of their choices, readily place blame, and are hesitant to offer credit. They might achieve their goals, but they create resentment and damaged relationships along the way. If you think your career has stagnated despite your achievements, this could be the hidden barrier holding you back. You are being "outvoted" in the informal, behind-the-scenes conversations that determine who is promoted. Your peers don't support you, and your subordinates lack confidence in you. Your leaders perceive you as a high-maintenance individual who cannot build and nurture a team. You are stuck because you haven't realized that sustainable success is a team sport, and as a result, you have alienated your entire team.

The Asset of Being Honorable: An honorable professional acts with integrity and respects others. They recognize that the way you achieve results matters just as much as the results themselves. They fiercely protect their team from outside criticism and generously and publicly share credit. They treat every person with dignity, regardless of their position or role. They uphold their word as a sacred bond. This doesn't make them soft; it makes them a leader people want to follow. This builds a strong and devoted network of allies who will support you, disseminate crucial information, and take pride in your accomplishments. Honor serves as the basis for authentic leadership and influence. This transforms you from a task manager into a respected leader. It paves the way for advancement.

The Growth Path from Callous to Honorable: The path from callous to honorable begins with shifting your focus from "me" to "we." During your next team meeting, prioritize recognizing the contributions of your team members. In the event of a team mistake, take the opportunity to acknowledge shared responsibility in public before addressing the issue privately. Create a list of the people who helped you on your last project and identify a specific, genuine way to thank each of them. These actions are deposits in the bank of goodwill. The results show a significant change in your operational methods. Former critics can become your supporters. This change can help you overcome the obstacles that have been holding you back.

8. Humble vs. 48. Conceited

The Liability of Being Conceited: The conceited professional is a dead end on the road of development. This is a key feature of the EgoOS, which runs a constant self-promotion script to protect and inflate its status. They are sure they are right, immune to criticism, and dismissive of new ideas.

This arrogance is the ultimate career staller because it makes learning and cooperation impossible. The world, your industry, and your company are all constantly evolving, but you remain static. You confuse your current knowledge with lasting understanding. This attitude makes it difficult for you to work with. It isolates you from colleagues who have stopped trying to collaborate with someone who thinks they know everything. You feel stuck because you are trapped by your ego, making it difficult to see new paths and opportunities that require learning and adaptation.

The Asset of Being Humble: True professional humility is not weakness or self-deprecation; it is a confident awareness of one's limitations. The humble professional is so secure in their abilities that they have nothing to prove. This allows them to be curious, receptive to coaching, and open to great ideas from any source. They seek diverse opinions and view constructive criticism as a valuable gift. This mindset makes them a learning machine, constantly strengthening their skills and changing their approach. Leaders view humility not as weakness but as a strong indication of growth potential. They recognize that a humble leader is resilient and practical, making them a reliable and intelligent choice for senior roles.

The Growth Path from Conceited to Humble: The antidote to conceit is intentional curiosity. For the next month, use the mantra: "What can I learn here?" After your next presentation, speak with a trusted colleague. Ask, "What is one thing I could have done better?" Focus on improvement instead of seeking compliments. During your next team brainstorming session, consider listening for the first 15 minutes before contributing your thoughts. Concentrate on listening instead. When someone questions your idea, respond with "Tell me more." Avoid being defensive. These actions reduce arrogance. They promote growth, insights, and connections that can advance your career.

9. Caring" vs. 49. "Uncaring

The Liability of Being Uncaring: The uncaring worker views the job as merely a business proposition. They ignore their team's morale, fail to notice a colleague's burnout, and are out of touch with the personal stories happening around them. This emotional indifference leads to a harsh and fragile team culture. People may comply, but they will not commit to it. Loyalty is nonexistent, and discretionary effort is a foreign concept. If your career has stalled, it may be due to a lack of emotional capital for leadership. Despite your efficiency, the absence of emotional intelligence could discourage others from collaborating with you. You are unable to advance because you cannot inspire the kind of followership that is essential for leading high-performing, resilient teams.

The Asset of Being Caring: A caring professional shows genuine empathy and cares about the well-being of their coworkers. They know that people drive all outcomes. The manager sees a team member struggling and softly asks, "Are you okay?" The coworkers step in to help when they notice a team member working, even if it is not their responsibility. This fosters a strong sense of psychological safety, making people feel valued as individuals, not just as workers. This care is not just charity; it is a smart leadership advantage. It creates strong loyalty, encourages deep involvement, and forms teams that can handle any challenge. As a caring professional, your colleagues will go above and beyond to support you, and this collective energy can help you overcome career stagnation.

The Growth Path from Uncaring to Caring: To show care, you should practice paying close attention. Start by learning one non-work-related fact about each person on your immediate team. Before launching into your agenda in a one-on-one, start with a simple, sincere, "How are you doing?" and listen to the answer. The next time you see a colleague achieve a small win, walk over to their desk and tell them you noticed. These are not grand gestures. They are small, consistent acts of human connection and kindness that build the trust and social capital necessary to be considered the leader you are meant to be.

10. Passionate vs. 50. Unmotivated

The Liability of Being Unmotivated: An unmotivated professional is the embodiment of career stagnation. The spark of motivation has vanished. The work has become a joyless series of obligations, and the "why" behind the effort has been forgotten. This lack of passion is not a private feeling; it is a public broadcast that demotivates everyone you work with. It manifests as a weighty sigh during a meeting, a sluggish tone in an email, and an evident lack of enthusiasm for a new initiative. You've transformed into a stagnant source of energy. Someone so invested in the present will never lead the future. You feel stuck, and you have given up emotionally and mentally.

The Asset of Being Passionate: A passionate worker feels deeply connected to a larger goal beyond their daily tasks. Their work reveals what they care about, and it generates genuine excitement. This passion fuels top performance. It offers the strength to overcome setbacks and the creativity to discover new solutions. This enthusiasm spreads easily, fostering belief and gathering support. It turns a group of people into a dedicated, mission-focused team. A passionate professional does not wait for instructions to excel; they are already leading the way, exploring new opportunities, and driving innovation. This demonstrates your readiness for more challenging tasks. Passion shows that you take ownership, identifying you as someone who creates value rather than merely managing tasks.

The Growth Path from Unmotivated to Passionate: To reignite passion, you must reconnect with your purpose. This is the peak of personal development. Take a moment to reflect on this question sincerely: What part of my work, if any, truly matters to me? If the answer is "nothing," you're in the wrong role, and no character change will help. But if you can find even a small spark like assisting a client in solving a complex problem or mentoring a junior colleague. Your job is to pour water on it. Volunteer for projects that align with that spark. Discuss the significance of the work during your team meetings. Connect your daily tasks back to that larger purpose. Passion involves aligning your energy with your values and the objectives of your employer.

In Conclusion

The ten key assets of the Being Pillar are vital for your Character OS. These essential elements are crucial, much like water for life. It is critical for professionals experiencing career stagnation. Despite your expertise, you may feel unnoticed and undervalued, which can lead to a sense of unrealized potential. This pillar is not just about self-improvement; it is the foundation that fights against stagnation, reduced visibility, and repetitive roles that keep you behind less qualified peers. This happens when your internal alignment shifts, weakening the discipline, integrity, and resilience needed to succeed. By carefully looking at each asset and liability—from bringing back confidence to fostering passion—you're not just changing habits. You are creating a major reset that brings back your inner voice and aligns your daily actions with your core values. Also, it rebuilds the confidence needed to seek the recognition and progress you deserve.

Investing in this reboot means facing the quiet ways stagnation shows up in your work life like the self-doubt that holds you back in meetings. Also, the indecision that slows down projects and weakens your leadership. Or the lack of enthusiasm that turns big goals into tedious tasks. All of these create a cycle of feeling undervalued and missing chances. Mid-career managers with stagnant salaries and experienced executives losing influence can find a way to regain purpose through this character-driven transformation. It includes reflective questions to explore your thoughts and growth paths to turn weaknesses into strengths. Also, practices to ensure your beliefs lead to consistent, impactful actions. As you strengthen the Being pillar, you will see some fundamental changes. First, increased energy to overcome setbacks. Second, honest self-talk that boosts confidence. Third, a humble but firm approach that enhances your visibility.

This journey is not about achieving perfection immediately; it is a continuous process grounded in evidence. It is for professionals like you who want to go beyond quick fixes and focus on the inner work needed for lasting success. By developing traits such as honor and passion, you will break through barriers that limit you and motivate others. You will create a positive impact that enhances teamwork and leads to new leadership opportunities. Use this reboot as a tool to overcome professional stagnation. Connect your identity with meaningful actions. Making your inner strengths the motivation for extraordinary achievements that far outweigh external circumstances or past frustrations.

This character reset helps you live your values. It turns doubt into strength. Making daily choices is vital for your influence and happiness. As you apply these principles, keep a record of your progress. Notice how setting new routines helps you focus. Discover how friendly interactions can help rebuild your connections. Pay attention to how getting involved again sparks your motivation. The Being pillar is as vital as water is to life. It's a force that helps you grow. It satisfies the need for real progress. This approach ensures that your career not only endures challenging periods but also grows stronger and creates a greater impact.

Ralph Waldo Emerson

"What lies within us is far more important than what lies behind and in front of us."

CHAPTER 7

The "Feeling" Pillar: Vital and Invisible Oxygen

Oscar Wilde

"Be yourself; everyone else is already taken."

Introduction

First, let us recognize your current situation. You are a driven and skilled professional, but it seems your career has hit a plateau. It feels like you are stuck, as if your steady progress has suddenly halted while everyone around you keeps moving forward. You put in significant effort, but it does not seem to be paying off. You feel like you are becoming less visible, and it is frustrating to feel ignored and unappreciated. You have encountered an invisible barrier, and you think the issue is not a lack of skills on your resume or a wrong strategy, but something more profound—your internal mindset.

You are correct. The key to shattering that invisible ceiling and rebooting your career lies in the one area most professionals are never formally trained to master: their capacity for *Feeling*. If your core identity—your *Being*—*is* the water, then your emotional intelligence is the oxygen. Without it, the most potent human being remains inert. When we ignore, misunderstand, or mismanage our emotional world, we create the very conditions of career stagnation that now frustrate you. We become emotionally suffocated—stuck, overwhelmed, and unable to move forward.

To truly thrive and regain traction, you must learn to master your emotional output. This mastery is known as emotional intelligence (EI), and it is not a mysterious gift, but a concrete set of skills that you can develop. It is the foundation of the character-driven reset you are seeking. EI begins with looking inward to understand what you are feeling, but it extends outward into how you project that feeling and interpret the feelings of others. It's the unseen force that determines whether you are perceived as a reliable future leader or a talented but risky contributor who cannot be trusted.

TABLE B

"Feeling" Character Assets (Momentum Builders)	"Feeling" Character Liabilities (Stagnation Anchors)
11. Attentive	51. Inattentive
12. Authentic	52. Phony
13. Empathetic	53. Apathetic
14. Forgiving	54. Resentful
15. Grateful	55. Complaintive
16. Loyal	56. Disloyal
17. Patient	57. Impatient
18. Respectful	58. Rude
19. Sociable	59. Unsociable
20. Trusting	60. Jealous

As author Daniel Goleman famously claimed, when it comes to long-term career success, your EI may be far more important than your IQ. We have all seen knowledgeable colleagues who remained isolated, unable to build the relationships necessary for influence. Conversely, we've seen leaders who weren't the most intelligent people in the room but could connect, inspire, and mobilize teams to achieve incredible results. That is the power of EI. It's the secret ingredient that turns professional inertia into reignited momentum.

This chapter will help you reset this vital aspect of your character's operating system. We will examine the 10 essential "Feeling" assets that can help you regain your influence, along with the 10 liabilities that are currently hindering your progress. This isn't about fixing something that's broken; it's about unlocking a more whole, effective, and deeply fulfilled version of yourself—a version whose career is no longer stuck but soaring.

What follows is not merely a list of positive and negative behaviors. For you, the professional experiencing stagnation, this is a diagnostic tool and a strategic roadmap. The invisible anchors weighing down your career, causing friction and distrust, are the "liabilities" listed below. The assets are the specific, actionable components of the character-driven reboot you need to restore traction, elevate your influence, and achieve sustained peak performance. Analyze each pair honestly, not just as workplace behavior, but as a direct cause of your current career plateau.

The Relational Balance Sheet

11. Attentive vs. 51. Inattentive

The Liability of Feeling Inattentive: Feeling or appearing inattentive broadcasts that you are not prepared for the next level of responsibility. This behavior extends beyond simple carelessness. Checking your phone during meetings or seeming disengaged sends a powerful signal to leadership about your lack of commitment. This is a primary reason why capable individuals are often excluded from promotions. Your lack of focus creates doubt about your ability to handle more complex duties, damaging trust and solidifying the invisible ceiling you're trying to break.

The Asset of Being Attentive: Being attentive is a clear demonstration of executive presence. When you put away devices, take helpful notes, and ask insightful questions, you show your profound engagement with the work. Referencing past discussions or acknowledging a colleague's input builds the relational capital that translates directly into professional influence. This practice is more than mere politeness; it is a strategic approach that restores trust and demonstrates your readiness for greater challenges, shifting you from being overlooked to being someone whose opinion is sought after.

The Journey from Inattentive to Attentive: Your journey to greater influence begins with the conscious choice to remain engaged in the present moment. Consider setting your phone aside when engaging in conversation or attending a meeting. Practice active listening. Take notes on what is said, as well as the context behind it. Before you submit your work, take a moment to review it? Look for minor mistakes because they can hurt your credibility. When you recall details from past talks, you demonstrate your value to the team. This helps you shift from being a source of frustration to a center of focus. It helps rebuild trust.

12. Authentic vs. 52. Phony

The Liability of Feeling Phony: A phony person builds a restrictive career environment. This behavior—saying one thing while doing another—is a core driver of career stagnation because it renders you unpredictable and untrustworthy. Praising teamwork but then taking individual credit or treating superiors with deference while being dismissive of peers creates a cloud of doubt around your character. Leaders are unwilling to advance individuals they cannot rely on to be consistent and reliable. This inauthenticity is a direct cause of your fading visibility and stalled momentum as people cease to depend on you.

The Asset of Feeling Authentic: An authentic character builds a reputation that paves the way for advancement. Authenticity, defined as the alignment of your values, words, and actions, serves as the foundation for a sustainable career climb. When you are genuine you own up to your mistakes, and keep your promises. You create a meaningful reputation. People will see you as reliable and authentic. This consistency builds a safe space and it helps others feel comfortable collaborating with you. You become the person everyone turns to for essential projects and leadership. You break down career barriers with each authentic interaction.

The Journey from Phony to Authentic: Start by taking a hard look at what you say and do. It is time to be real. If you believe in teamwork, make sure to acknowledge your colleagues' contributions publicly first. Always treat everyone with respect for it doesn't matter what their role is. When you make a mistake, take full responsibility for it. Don't make excuses. This path isn't about sharing every personal thought. It's about staying true to your values in all you say and do. This journey establishes a reputation for reliability. This reputation serves as the foundation for long-term career growth and success.

13. Empathetic vs. 53. Apathetic

The Liability of Feeling Apathetic: Apathy reinforces career stagnation by signaling a profound lack of investment in teamwork and collaboration. When you focus exclusively on your tasks and ignore the struggles of your colleagues, you are perceived as disconnected and self-serving. Your minimal engagement in team celebrations or collaborative efforts shows a lack of commitment to shared success. This is the reason many skilled professionals see their careers stagnate; others perceive them as mere cogs, rather than as potential leaders capable of inspiring a team. This disposition erodes trust and prevents the formation of meaningful connections, leaving you isolated and easily overlooked.

The Asset of Feeling Empathetic: Empathy is a strong skill and it helps create the teamwork needed for success. It can turn a group of people into a loyal and high-performing team. When you see a coworker feeling overwhelmed, offering help or just listening can make a big difference. It creates a safe space for everyone. This is how you elevate your influence far beyond your official job description. People become willing to go the extra mile for you in return. This supportive behavior helps reduce friction at work and fosters strong relationships. These relationships are crucial for navigating significant challenges and securing the attention necessary to succeed.

The Journey from Apathetic to Empathetic: To shift from apathy, you must make the human element of your work a conscious priority. Actively watch for nonverbal signs of stress in your colleagues and be ready to help without judgment. Demonstrate your appreciation for your coworkers as individuals by participating in team events. Even a simple act, like helping with a small task when someone is busy, can dramatically improve team dynamics. You will transform from a solo contributor into a force multiplier whose support elevates the entire group, making your advancement a natural outcome of the team's success.

14. Forgiving vs. 54. Resentful

The Liability of Feeling Resentful: Holding onto resentment poisons your professional effectiveness and holds your team captive to the past. This bitterness manifests in obvious ways, such as passive-aggressive remarks or the deliberate avoidance of certain colleagues. Constantly bringing up past failures in meetings does not signal that you are detail-oriented; it signals that you are an obstacle to progress. This behavior is a career anchor, branding you as difficult to work with and preventing the collaborative synergy required for the most exciting and career-defining projects.

The Asset of Feeling Forgiveness: A forgiving mindset propels team momentum forward. When you release grievances and frame mistakes as collective learning opportunities, you cultivate an environment of trust and innovation. This is a clear indicator of strong leadership. When you calmly discuss problems and seek solutions instead of blaming others, you foster stronger relationships. This also helps people feel safe to take creative risks. Colleagues will feel safe admitting errors and proposing bold ideas in your presence. This approach transforms potential conflicts into moments of growth, establishing you as a catalyst for progress and an obvious candidate for leadership.

The Journey from Resentful to Forgiving: Transform resentment into a strategic asset by intentionally reframing mistakes as data for future success. When a conflict happens, try to stay calm and respectful. Focus on finding solutions instead of blaming others. Avoid revisiting previously resolved issues. Focus on the present instead. This deliberate shift from bitterness to forward-looking problem-solving will not only improve your state of mind but also enhance your overall well-being. Still, it will also cement your reputation as a stable, mature leader who can guide a team through any challenge, thereby restoring your upward career path.

15. Grateful vs. 55. Complaintive

The Liability of Feeling Complaintive: A complaining attitude actively repels opportunity. Focusing too much on problems and grievances can hurt team morale. It saps your energy and motivation. When you concentrate on a minor error in a successful project or ignore the support from those around you, it reflects a belief that nothing is truly satisfactory. This behavior can harm your career. Your colleagues might start to pull away. Managers may view you as a problem rather than a solution. This could mean you're the last person they think of for essential projects.

The Asset of Feeling Grateful: A grateful disposition attracts collaboration and success. In the professional world, gratitude is expressed through the active and specific acknowledgment of others' contributions. It goes beyond a simple "thank you" to publicly highlighting a teammate's excellent idea or sending a note to a mentor about how their advice made a real difference. When people feel truly recognized and appreciated, they are more likely to give their best effort to the projects you work on. This shifts the whole vibe of your team. It puts you at the center of a positive and successful atmosphere.

The Journey from Complaintive to Grateful: To make the change, you need to practice noticing and saying the good things on purpose. Make it a daily habit to see three things your coworkers did well. Instead of just criticizing, try to give honest and specific compliments. Turn feelings of entitlement into appreciation. Recognize the hard work of those who help you. This shift in perspective will enhance your work environment. This change can shift the atmosphere from being tense to inspiring. People will feel motivated to help you reach your goals because you are willing to help them with theirs.

16. Loyal vs. 56. Disloyal

The Liability of Feeling Disloyal: Disloyalty is an act of career self-sabotage. Behaviors such as taking undue credit for a team's work, sharing confidential information, or undermining a project after agreeing to support it erode trust and confidence in the individual. Speaking negatively about teammates or the company creates a toxic environment that stifles honest communication. This could potentially result in a career plateau or even dismissal. It shows a fundamental flaw in your character. No leader will trust someone who puts their own goals above the team's success. This can leave you feeling alone and without the support you need to move forward.

The Asset of Feeling Loyal: A loyal character builds trust. It's essential for the whole team. Loyalty means standing by your colleagues. It's about supporting them, even when they're not around. You should also keep your promises. If you make a promise, keep it. Follow through on what you said you would do. When faced with challenges, you work together to solve problems. It is not about blaming anyone. This reliability builds trust. Team members feel secure in taking creative risks. Your loyalty demonstrates your trustworthiness as a leader. That makes you a great choice to lead an important project or team.

The Journey from Disloyal to Loyal: You can actively build loyalty by making collective success your top priority. Make it a habit to support your colleagues' work in public and to address negative gossip promptly. When projects succeed, award credit to the team; when they fail, guide the conversation toward solutions. Let your word be your bond by following through on every promise. This change in focus moves away from personal gain. It emphasizes strong team support. This builds deep trust, which is crucial for career growth.

17. Patient vs. 57. Impatient:

The Liability of Feeling Impatient: Impatience creates chaos and signals an inability to lead effectively. This is the EgoOS expressing frustration when delays or obstacles thwart its core directive for rapid ascent. Constant interruptions, visible signs of frustration in meetings, and rapid-fire demands for updates do not convey urgency; they represent a lack of trust in your team and a lack of control over your emotions. This behavior leads to rushed work, resulting in lower quality and discouraging colleagues from speaking up. It cultivates a stressful, high-anxiety atmosphere where people fear asking questions or admitting mistakes. This is a significant setback for your career. It shows you struggle with the uncertainty and pressure that come with responsible positions.

The Asset of Feeling Patient: Patience shows how steady a true leader can be. It demonstrates their emotional strength. Staying calm when things get tough helps you think better. It's important when things don't turn out as expected. When you take the time to listen before speaking, your coworkers will feel valued and respected. This respect helps create open conversations. Those conversations can lead to better results. Assisting a team in finding a solution rather than simply providing instructions strengthens their critical thinking. It also provides them with a sense of ownership. This method creates a calm and supportive environment, fostering trust and creativity. You become the steady person everyone relies on during tough times.

The Journey from Impatient to Patient: Being patient can help you handle your feelings more effectively. When you want to react, stop for a moment. Take a deep breath before speaking or acting. Train yourself to listen attentively to others, waiting until they have finished speaking before responding. Purge frustrated gestures and demanding language from your communications. Instead of demanding answers, work alongside your team to identify roadblocks and develop solutions together. This journey transforms you from a source of stress into a source of stability, a key trait for any aspiring leader.

18. Respectful vs. 58. Rude

The Liability of Feeling Rude: Being rude at work will harm your professional relationships. Dismissive comments, constant interruptions, and ignoring simple manners all take a toll on how people see you. It causes friction, making colleagues hesitant to collaborate, share ideas, or be supportive of you. This behavior does not show authority. Instead, it shows a lack of emotional control and self-awareness. Decision-makers might view you as a risk. They might believe that they cannot trust you to represent the team or company in crucial situations. This could limit your chances for advancement.

The Asset of Feeling Respectful: Respect is what gives you influence. Treating everyone with respect is essential. It doesn't matter who they are or what their title is. This makes a safe place for everyone. People feel valued in your presence, making them more willing to contribute their best ideas and discretionary effort. This consistent show of respect fosters open communication, builds powerful alliances, and marks you as a mature, centered leader who is capable of guiding diverse teams with effectiveness and grace.

The Journey from Rude to Respectful: Change begins with understanding how we connect with others. Commit to listening. Don't plan your response while someone else is talking. Recognize the value in other people's views, even if you disagree. Replace dismissive language with inclusive phrasing and become more aware of your nonverbal cues. Practice simple, consistent courtesies, such as saying "please" and "thank you." This shift will change your professional identity from an abrasive obstacle to a respected collaborator, reopening the path for your career to move forward.

19. Sociable vs. 59. Unsociable

The Liability of Feeling Unsociable: Chronic isolation at work constructs an invisible wall around your career. This manifests as consistently skipping team lunches, avoiding all non-task conversations, and being unapproachable. This unsociability suggests that you would rather not be part of the team, even when you're present. It prevents the formation of the informal networks and alliances that are crucial for organizational visibility and support. As time passes, people tend to overlook you for collaborative projects and leadership roles that require strong interpersonal skills, which can lead to feelings of being an outsider.

The Asset of Feeling Sociable: Being sociable drives professional networking and real teamwork. Connecting with coworkers on a personal level helps build trust and rapport. This goes beyond just meeting project deadlines. You can learn about how your team works and also collect informal information. Additionally, you can build a group of supporters who will stand by your side. You don't need to be an extrovert; just be friendly and genuinely interested in others. This networking is essential, and it helps you grow your influence. It also opens up opportunities you might not notice otherwise.

The Journey from Unsociable to Sociable: This journey begins with small, steady steps. Be sure to attend the next team social event. Even if you can only stay for a brief while, it's essential to be there. Discuss a coworker's weekend with them and show genuine interest when they share their experiences. Take five minutes to engage with those seated near you before putting on your headphones. The goal is to go beyond just being there, and it is about really connecting with others. When you create small connections, you break down the walls of loneliness and separation. This helps you become part of the influence and opportunities in your organization.

10. Trusting vs. 60. Jealousy

The Liability of Feeling Jealous: Professional jealousy can harm your team and your career. It is a direct symptom of the EgoOS, which is fueled by a constant comparison engine that assesses your status against others. It often shows up when someone undermines a colleague's success, keeps information to themselves, or questions others' motives. It shows deep insecurity and a scarcity mindset. This means believing that someone else's success takes away from your own. This behavior hinders teamwork and creates a toxic environment marked by suspicion. It can also damage your reputation. Leaders will not promote someone who appears more interested in competing with others than in collaborating to achieve a common goal.

The Asset of Feeling Trusting: A trusting nature comes from self-confidence. This is what defines a collaborative leader. When you celebrate your colleagues' successes and believe they mean well, you create a safe and positive environment. When you delegate important tasks and share information freely, you show that you trust in your team's competence. This method fosters mutual understanding and creates strong partnerships. You become a reliable leader who lifts others.

The Journey from Jealousy to Trusting: This critical transition requires a conscious shift from a scarcity mindset to one of abundance. Begin by acknowledging a coworker's achievement. You can either do this in public or send them a private message to congratulate them. If you are feeling jealous, consider it an opportunity to gain insight from that person's achievements. Consider letting go of some control. Consider allowing a coworker to handle a task that you typically handle. When you actively decide to trust in and appreciate the combined power of your team, you shift from being a cautious rival to a reliable and impactful center of teamwork.

In Conclusion

This pillar gives your character real emotional strength. It connects what you believe inside to what happens outside. For the professional whose career has flatlined, mastering this pillar is not optional; it is the core work of your career reboot. It is how you develop the emotional intelligence (EI) that will allow you to understand others, read situations with clarity, and create a genuine impact.

Your technical skills and experience got you to this point, but they are no longer enough. At this stage of your career, EI is a great differentiator.

The 10 Feeling assets we've explored—attentiveness, authenticity, empathy, forgiveness, gratitude, loyalty, patience, respect, sociability, and trust—are the Feeling tools for your character-driven reset. Without these traits, people may respect your work, but they won't trust, follow, or support you. Without trust and empathy, a leader cannot motivate a team to achieve remarkable feats that garner attention from the entire professional environment.

What can we expect from an emotionally intelligent and authentic leader? They make a real difference. They reignite momentum, and they elevate influence. Their legacy is built not just on their achievements but on the people they lift. When you practice forgiveness, your team becomes more resilient. When you demonstrate gratitude, you improve the entire culture. When you trust others, working together becomes easy and strong. These emotional strengths give you the decisive edge needed to shatter the invisible ceiling and turn stagnation into sustained, deeply fulfilling success. Success is not just what you do; it's the trust you build, the good energy you create, and the lasting impact you have on others. That is how you get your career back on track.

Aaron Judge

"If your team is in the trenches, you have to be in the trenches with them."

CHAPTER 8

The "Doing" Pillar: A Real and Meaningful Environment

Henry Ford

"You can't build your reputation on what you are going to do."

Introduction

You have journeyed inward, recalibrating your core identity—your *Being*—and mastered the emotional currents that define your influence—your *Feeling*. Now, we arrive at the third and most visible pillar of your character-driven reboot: *Doing*. This is where your internal reset becomes external proof. If *Being* is the engine's design and *Feeling* is the oxygen, then *Doing* is the traction that grips the road and produces forward momentum. For you, the professional whose career has hit an invisible wall, this is the most critical stage. People see your talent and ambition. However, they are now watching to see how consistently you can deliver results.

Feeling stuck in your career can be frustrating. It often happens when what you want to do does not align with what you are actually doing. You may feel committed, yet your actions are perceived as indifferent. You may have a vision, but your daily focus appears shortsighted. This is the gap where trust erodes, where visibility fades, and where leaders hesitate to offer you the next level of responsibility. They closely monitor not only your promises but also your daily actions. Your actions are the data they use to determine your future.

This pillar is not about working harder; it's about working with demonstrable results. Your accountability, the promises you keep, and the deadlines you meet demonstrate your ability to deliver. Getting the hang of the "Doing" pillar is what turns you from just a capable team member into an essential leader. It involves transitioning from a perceived risk to a dependable, trusted individual capable of addressing the organization's most significant challenges. By transforming your refreshed character into steady, decisive actions, you will demonstrate clear evidence that you are prepared to overcome your current limitations and spark new growth in your career.

What follows is your roadmap for translating character into tangible results. These are not merely habits; they are the gears of your professional engine. For you, the stalled professional, the "liabilities" are the patterns of action—or inaction—that have ground your career to a halt by destroying productivity, trust and credibility. However, the "assets" are the specific, powerful behaviors that will rebuild that trust and restore your reputation for excellence. They provide the undeniable proof of your readiness for a greater role. Examine each pair not as a behavioral preference, but as a direct lever for your career reboot.

TABLE C

"Doing" Character Assets (Momentum Builders)	"Doing" Character Liabilities (Stagnation Traps)
21. Accountable	61. Unreliable
22. Deferential	62. Arrogant
23. Dependable	63. Undependable

24. Diligent	64. Lazy
25. Organized	65. Disorganized
26. Punctual	66. Tardy
27. Responsible	67. Irresponsible
28. Tactful	68. Reckless
29. Thorough	69. Sloppy
30. Tolerant	70. Intolerant

The Action Balance Sheet

21. Accountable vs. 61. Unreliable

The Liability of Being Unreliable: If you are unreliable, leaders will see you as a risky choice. This can stop you from moving forward. Missing deadlines, making excuses, or blaming others hurts trust. Trust is key to moving forward. When colleagues and managers cannot count on you to deliver on your promises, they stop giving you meaningful work. This is the reason many skilled professionals find themselves in a bind. Some perceive them as talented but unpredictable, necessitating constant review or preparation of backup plans. Your reputation as an unreliable team member will likely result in your exclusion from high-profile projects, which will hinder your career advancement.

The Asset of Being Accountable: Being accountable shows that you take ownership and also signals that you are ready to lead. When you take responsibility for your actions and decisions, you create a strong reputation. This includes both the positive and negative outcomes. Instead of hiding problems, you bring them to light with a proposed solution. This behavior creates an environment of psychological safety and makes you a stabilizing force on your team. Leaders entrust their most critical initiatives to those they know will own the results, making accountability the key that unlocks greater responsibility and influence.

The Journey from Unreliable to Accountable: The journey to accountability begins with the radical decision to take complete ownership of your outcomes. You remove blame and excuses from your vocabulary. If a deadline might be at risk, communicate it early and provide a plan to mitigate the impact. Should you make a mistake, acknowledge it. Consider what went wrong, then explain how you'll fix it and stop it from happening again. This is not about being perfect. It is about creating strong trust. This change turns you from someone unreliable into an accountable person. It helps restore the confidence you need to advance in your career.

22. Deferential vs. 62. Arrogant

The Liability of Being Arrogant: An arrogant professional exhibits an undeserved sense of superiority and often overlooks the ideas and efforts of those around them. This kind of behavior manifests as a dismissive attitude, which can create tension and damage work relationships. Being arrogant can significantly hinder teamwork because it prevents people from speaking openly and sharing their thoughts, which can create a hostile work atmosphere. It can substantially harm the person involved, tarnishing their reputation and making it more challenging for them to lead effectively.

The Asset of Being Deferential: A deferential professional values their superiors, colleagues, and clients, fostering a positive and harmonious workplace atmosphere. They value the experience and insights of others, which promotes collaboration and mutual respect. Such people are often respectful of different points of view. Showing respect and consideration fosters a workplace where everyone feels valued and recognized for their contributions. This can make people feel more positive at work, lift their moods, and ultimately help the entire team work better together. It fosters open discussions, knowledge sharing, and the establishment of solid professional connections.

The Journey from Arrogant to Deferential: Transforming from arrogance to deferential requires a self-examination and a readiness to embrace change. It starts with understanding how arrogance can harm relationships and affect teamwork. It is vital for a person to actively seek feedback from their peers and be willing to listen to constructive suggestions for improvement. This could mean working on your listening skills, showing understanding towards others, and appreciating what everyone brings to the table. This process requires us to change our way of thinking, emphasizing teamwork, respect, and the understanding that everyone brings something meaningful to the table. By regularly demonstrating humility, respecting others' viewpoints, and being open to learning, a person can gradually change their behavior and cultivate a more deferential attitude.

23. Dependable vs. 63. Undependable

The Liability of Being Undependable: An undependable professional is inconsistent, which results in unmet expectations and a loss of trust. This unreliability frequently manifests as broken promises, missed deadlines, and a general lack of follow-through. All of which can severely damage an individual's professional reputation. Undependability significantly undermines collaboration, breeds inefficiencies, and erodes the confidence colleagues place in that person. Consequently, their actions often put the entire team in a difficult position, creating stress and requiring others to compensate for their actions.

The Asset of Being Dependable: A dependable professional is an individual you can rely on to complete tasks on time and meet expectations while consistently demonstrating excellent performance and behavior. These individuals can be relied upon to keep their promises and deliver outstanding results, making them a vital part of any team. Their reliability, consistent performance, and dedication to their responsibilities foster trust and reduce stress for both teammates and supervisors, leading to a more stable and productive workplace.

The Journey from Undependable to Dependable: Changing from being undependable to becoming dependable is a process that requires intentional effort and a commitment to excellence. It begins by understanding how being undependable can harm trust and team performance. Noting that failing to keep commitments and missing deadlines have detrimental effects. This calls for a fundamental change in how we approach things—focusing on planning, being realistic about what we can achieve, and sticking closely to our schedules and tasks. This involves developing solid organizational skills and prioritizing tasks according to their importance. Additionally, addressing potential problems or delays ahead of time is crucial for establishing a reputation for dependability.

24. Diligent vs. 64. Lazy

The Liability of Being Lazy: A lazy professional is characterized by an avoidance of effort or exertion in their work, frequently leading to unfinished tasks and a failure to meet expectations. This inertia often manifests as procrastination, a noticeable lack of motivation, and a reluctance to take on more responsibilities. This significantly hinders productivity. When people are lazy, it can really hurt how well the team works together. This creates an unfair situation in which some individuals contribute more than others, potentially lowering the morale of everyone involved. Additionally, this ongoing avoidance of responsibilities undermines trust between colleagues and supervisors, significantly harming the person's professional image and reliability in the work environment.

The Asset of Being Diligent: The diligent individual tackles their tasks with steady determination and consistent effort, staying strong especially when challenges arise. Their strong work ethic really stands out, marked by a keen attention to detail in everything they do. They have a genuine commitment to ensuring customer satisfaction, as they consistently strive to put forth their best effort to achieve their objectives. This commitment guarantees the creation of top-notch outcomes, establishing them as a dependable foundation for any group. Diligence fosters a reputation for dependability and reduces stress for collaborators by ensuring tasks are completed thoroughly and on time. It is critical to uphold high standards and achieve collective success.

The Journey from Lazy to Diligent: Transitioning from being lazy to developing a strong work ethic is a significant shift that requires a real commitment and the establishment of new habits. It begins with acknowledging and facing the habit of shying away from effort and the drawbacks of procrastination, which can lead to failing to meet our goals. This journey involves cultivating self-discipline, breaking big tasks into smaller, more manageable steps, and setting practical, achievable goals to create momentum. Focusing on what matters and managing tasks wisely. It is dedicating ourselves to doing things right and with care. When you put in the effort, stick to your promises, and take your responsibilities seriously, you can gradually earn a reputation for being diligent and become a reliable and effective team member.

25. Organized vs. 65. Disorganized

The Liability of Being Disorganized: A disorganized professional often finds it really tough to keep track of their time, tasks, and resources. This can lead to inefficiencies and cause them to miss deadlines more frequently. This chaos often manifests as a messy workspace and trouble managing time. Additionally, there is a constant struggle to prioritize tasks, which ultimately leads to a noticeable decline in productivity. Being disorganized can significantly contribute to your stress and make it difficult to accomplish even routine tasks. It also leaves a negative impression on your bosses and coworkers, which can lead to mistakes, unfinished tasks, and a decline in the team's effectiveness. When things are disorganized, it can significantly disrupt how everyone works together, disrupt project schedules, and undermine the collective effort of the whole team.

The Asset of Being Organized: A well-organized professional handles their tasks clearly and systematically, which helps them achieve excellent efficiency and maintain a tidy work environment. Keeping things organized helps manage time more effectively and complete tasks more accurately. People who are organized can focus more effectively on what needs to be done. They avoid those stressful last-minute scrambles and produce work that is both detailed and dependable. This skill builds a reputation for being trustworthy and reduces the likelihood of mistakes. It also fosters easier teamwork, making them a valuable and reliable team member.

The Journey from Disorganized to Organized: Transitioning from disorganization to a professional mindset requires a deliberate shift in habits and mindset, emphasizing the importance of structure and planning. It begins by acknowledging the problems and drawbacks associated with being disorganized, such as missing deadlines and lower productivity. A person must focus on developing strong time management skills, learning how to prioritize tasks effectively, and establishing systems to keep both their physical and digital workspaces organized. This involves breaking down large projects into smaller, manageable tasks and setting specific objectives. Also, establishing habits that help keep things under control and on track. By using these strategies, taking charge of your tasks, and staying dedicated to being organized and structured, you can change from someone who struggles with organization into a reliable and effective professional.

26. Punctual vs. 66. Tardy

The Liability of Being Tardy: A person who is often late to meetings, deadlines, or tasks tends to erode trust and cause numerous unnecessary problems. This usually manifests as being late, struggling with time management, or not adhering to set schedules, all of which contribute to a less professional vibe. Being late can significantly disrupt the workflow, making tasks more challenging for teammates. It also potentially damages your professional reputation by creating a negative impression over time. Furthermore, this behavior can lead to missed opportunities and a general decline in team productivity. Others may have to wait or reassign tasks to compensate for the delay.

The Asset of Being Punctual: A punctual professional consistently arrives on time and meets deadlines, demonstrating a profound respect for others' time and schedules. This unwavering adherence to timeliness not only signifies a high degree of reliability but also actively enhances workflow and projects a very professional image. Punctual individuals reduce disruptions and foster a more organized work environment. They improve overall team efficiency by meeting tasks and commitments as expected. Punctuality fosters essential trust among colleagues and superiors. It enables them to rely on timely contributions, which are fundamental for achieving collective goals and maintaining smooth operations.

The Journey from Tardy to Punctual: Changing from being someone who is consistently late to a person who shows up on time requires added focus. It is essential to develop self-discipline and genuinely appreciate the value of time. It begins with realizing how being late can negatively impact everything around us. It disrupts the workflow, creates issues for others, and can hurt how people perceive you. This change is all about developing strong time management skills. This may involve using calendars, setting reminders in advance, and carefully planning tasks and travel to allow for extra time in case of unexpected delays. Recognizing that being on time shows respect for your coworkers and dedication to professional standards is critical. By always being on time, taking charge of personal schedules, and avoiding procrastination, a person can establish a solid reputation as a reliable and punctual team player.

27. Responsible vs. 67. Irresponsible

The Liability of Being Irresponsible: Irresponsibility at work means being careless. It involves missing details and failing to consider the consequences of your actions. This shows up as messy work that others have to correct. This behavior also indicates a lack of concern for company resources and a failure to keep promises. This behavior can lead to career stagnation and shows a lack of respect for both the work and the team. It forces managers to seek to micromanage you. This breaks down trust with your coworkers. No organization will promote someone who makes more work for others. They need to trust that person to meet basic standards of quality and care.

The Asset of Being Responsible: A responsible professional takes ownership of their work. They make good decisions in everything they do. You treat company resources as if they were your own. You do your work carefully and accurately. You contemplate how your choices will affect others before you act. Being responsible shows a strong sign of leadership potential. It is a quiet yet essential quality, demonstrating that you can be trusted to work with minimal supervision. It also shows you care about doing a great job, not just finishing tasks. Your good reputation for being responsible helps you gain independence and the trust needed for essential tasks.

The Journey from Irresponsible to Responsible: Building good habits helps you become a responsible and professional individual. Before submitting your work, take a moment to review it and check for any errors.

Ensure it meets a high standard of quality. Before acting, review how it will impact your team and the business in the long term. Ensure that you honor every commitment, regardless of its size, challenge, and importance. This journey is about cultivating a mindset of deep care and responsibility. This change will turn you from someone who needs guidance into someone others trust to guide and to do a good job.

28. Tactful vs. 68. Reckless

The Liability of Being Reckless: A reckless professional acts without considering the potential dangers or consequences of their actions, which leads to risks and often results in adverse outcomes. This behavior is frequently characterized by taking unnecessary risks or ignoring established safety procedures. You make impulsive choices, all of which can place yourself and others in precarious situations. Recklessness fundamentally erodes trust, can tarnish a company's reputation, and may lead to accidents or legal complications. Such actions can significantly disrupt professional settings and may result in serious consequences for both the individual involved and the organization as a whole.

The Asset of Being Tactful: A skilled and tactful professional knows how to communicate thoughtfully and with care. It ensures that they avoid offending anyone and consistently show respect for others' feelings. This thoughtful approach helps foster better working relationships by promoting understanding and respect among team members. When people show care in their communication, it helps create a more friendly and productive atmosphere. When we communicate with each other with care and respect for everyone, we enhance our interactions and foster stronger cooperation.

The Journey from Reckless to Tactful: Switching from being reckless to being more tactful requires a significant shift in how we perceive our actions and their impact on those around us. It begins by acknowledging the genuine dangers and negative consequences that can result from making impulsive decisions or acting without careful consideration. Your choices can put you and others at risk, damaging your trust, reputation, and relationships. This journey is about self-control and developing the habit of pausing to consider the consequences of our actions. Being understanding, paying close attention, and learning how to communicate with others are essential components of this growth. By consistently applying these principles, a person can transition from creating uncomfortable situations to establishing positive and secure professional encounters.

29. Thorough vs. 69. Sloppy

The Liability of Being Sloppy: A sloppy professional is characterized by a notable lack of care and attention to detail in their work. It consistently results in untidy, careless, and inaccurate outputs that significantly lower established standards. This manifests as unfinished tasks, repeated errors, and noticeable disorganization, all of which significantly impact the quality of their contributions. People's lack of care can lead to mistakes that require correction and a redo. This might hurt the reputation of both the individual and the company. Additionally, sloppiness can lead to teammates needing to spend extra time and energy fixing or completing tasks, which interrupts the group's flow and can create feelings of frustration.

The Asset of Being Thorough: A thorough professional meticulously pays close attention to every detail, ensuring that all tasks are completed both thoroughly and accurately. The result is high-quality work. These individuals pay close attention to details and are dedicated to getting things exactly right, which makes their work reliable and of the highest quality. Being thorough enhances the quality of what each person contributes and helps establish a solid reputation for reliability and professionalism. This method also reduces the likelihood of mistakes and the need to repeat tasks. This considerate approach fosters trust among colleagues and their managers, ensuring that everyone can rely on the work being completed accurately and comprehensively.

The Journey from Sloppy to Thorough: To develop a thorough perspective, it is essential to think beyond your everyday tasks and responsibilities. Take some time to explore the latest trends in your industry and other related areas. In every project, ask yourself and your team, "What is our main goal?" How does this help us reach our long-term goals? Talk about the reasons for tasks, not just the steps to do them. This journey is about learning to think ahead. It's about seeing the bigger picture. This change in how you see things will turn you from a good doer into a great leader.

30. Tolerant vs. 70. Intolerant

The Liability of Being Intolerant: Showing intolerance at work, such as favoritism or unfair judgment, makes the workplace toxic. It can hurt careers and make things difficult for everyone. This behavior pushes colleagues away. It makes people feel unsafe and stops them from sharing ideas. It shows a closed mind and unfairness. These traits do not fit within today's professional environment. A person with intolerance cannot create or lead a diverse, high-performing team. Leaders will see you as a source of conflict. They may view you as a legal risk. This can disqualify you from roles that need fair and inclusive decision-making.

The Asset of Being Tolerant: Tolerance is vital for leaders. It means being open to different views and people. This quality helps build strong connections. A tolerant professional makes a welcoming space. Here, everyone feels respected. They can share their best ideas without fear and listen to different opinions. Logic rather than personal preferences guides your choices. This skill enables you to leverage the strengths of a diverse team. It leads to better problem-solving and more innovation. You appear to be a fair and mature leader. You can bring people together instead of pushing them apart.

The Journey from Intolerant to Tolerant: Becoming more tolerant takes self-awareness and effort. Try to hear what your colleagues think. Talk to people who have different backgrounds and views from you. When you make a quick judgment, take a moment to think. Ask yourself what assumptions are behind it. Try to see things from other people's perspectives. This helps you understand why they behave the way they do. We want to change unconscious intolerance into conscious inclusion. This path will help you become a better leader. It will also expand your view. You will grow wiser and more understanding in your work.

In Conclusion

The "Doing" pillar is all about how your actions define who you are to others and to your profession. It transforms your values and emotional abilities into something you can really grasp and demonstrate. People can observe it, quantify it, and have confidence in it. Your Being is your base. Your Feeling creates connections. But it is your Doing that proves it. For the professional fighting to regain momentum, your actions are the only currency that truly matters.

This is how you shatter the invisible ceiling. Your reputation is not built on your potential but on the accumulated evidence of your daily decisions. The consistency of your discipline, the integrity of your accountability, and the foresight of your proactivity are what superiors, peers, and clients observe. These are not soft skills; they are the concrete evidence of your leadership readiness. They build the trust that unlocks opportunities and creates the psychological safety required for teams to innovate and excel.

Bad habits, such as being unreliable, careless, or undependable, can harm your work. They also lower your team's morale and trust. It suggests that you prioritize your own interests over those of the group. They are the things you put on yourself that hold your career back. When you choose to act responsibly, stay committed, and have a clear vision, you can drive growth. It's not about being perfect. It's about taking responsibility. It is about creating a productive work environment, one step at a time. People will remember you for the actions you take. Every day, take steps to become the leader you aspire to be.

Billy Graham

"When wealth is lost, nothing is lost; when health is lost, something is lost; when character is lost, all is lost."

CHAPTER 9

THE "BECOMING" PILLAR: DYNAMIC & FORWARD-MOVING ENERGY

Nelson Mandela

"Resentment is like drinking poison and then hoping it will kill your enemies."

Introduction

What will remain when your career is over? What story will your presence tell, beyond just job titles and finished projects? Will people remember you as someone on whom they could rely? Or as a leader who changed a team, an industry, or a community for the better?

So far, we have explored the internal compass of Being, the emotional intelligence of Feeling, and the steadfast reliability of Doing. These pillars define who you are and how you act in the present. But Becoming is different. It is the dynamic energy that pulls you forward. It's about growing on purpose. It's about making changes that matter. You are in charge of your leadership path and future. The Doing pillar focuses on being consistent. The Becoming pillar is all about making progress. It marks the shift from managing your current responsibilities to creating future opportunities, not asking, "How am I performing?" But "What enduring influence will I have?"

To accomplish this, one needs a vision that extends beyond the present moment. Keep in mind your ascent can be cut short by the liabilities of this pillar—fear, pessimism, and greed act as subtle "circuit breakers," halting your progress before it can truly begin. They whisper that the future is too daunting or that your potential is fixed. This chapter will help you learn how to override them. We will look at the key parts of Becoming—courage, creativity, wisdom, and prudence. These are not just ideas. They are valuable tools. These virtues help you dream big. They turn your vision into reality. They also help you create a lasting legacy.

What follows is not just a list of virtues; it is a strategic blueprint for your future self. For you, the professional who is determined to break free from stagnation, the liabilities described here are the final, subtle anchors holding you back from a future of influence and purpose. The assets are the specific, actionable mindsets required to not only reboot your career but also to build a lasting legacy. Consider each pair as a distinct concept. Think of it as a choice. You can choose a future where things fade away or one where they stay relevant.

TABLE D

"Becoming" Character Assets (Legacy Builders)	"Becoming" Character Liabilities (Stagnation Traps)
31. Courageous	71. Fainthearted
32. Creative	72. Unimaginative
33. Adaptable	73. Inflexible
34. Focused	74. Procrastinate
35. Generous	75. Greedy

36. Just	76. Unjust
37. Optimistic	77. Pessimistic
38. Persuasive	78. Dissuasive
39. Prudent	79. Wasteful
40. Wise	80. Foolish

The Visionary's Balance Sheet

31. Courageous vs. 71. Fainthearted

The Liability of Feeling Fainthearted: Being fainthearted is a big reason why people go unnoticed in their jobs. Fear can hold you back. This isn't just general anxiety; it's a specific background script run by EgoOS—the fear of being overlooked, the fear of insignificance. It stops you from speaking up in important meetings. It makes you hesitate to volunteer for challenging projects. It makes you hesitate to volunteer for challenging projects. It even prevents you from questioning a poor strategy. Leadership sees this hesitation as a sign of weakness. They believe it reveals a lack of confidence and an inability to handle pressure. When you consistently listen to others or choose the easy route, it indicates that you've reached a plateau in your career. This makes it harder to break free from that plateau you want to leave behind.

The Asset of Being Courageous: Courage drives visibility and is also essential for effective leadership. It shows not by being fearless, but by acting with purpose even when afraid. When you dare to support a great idea, advocate for your team, or embrace a wise risk, you transform the way others perceive you. It is time to act and not just watch from the sidelines. It is your turn to take charge of what comes next. To break the invisible ceiling, don't wait for confirmation. Demonstrate your ability to take the lead, even in challenging situations.

The Journey from Fainthearted to Courageous: We begin this transformation by reevaluating risk in a new light. Begin with small, careful steps. Try to go just a bit beyond what feels comfortable. Share a thoughtful, different opinion during a small team meeting. Take on a task in a big project. Choose something you can do, even if it seems scary. Every small act of courage helps you gain confidence, and it affects how you respond to fear. It is time to face challenges head-on. Instead, you view them as chances to grow. They demonstrate that you are prepared for what comes next.

32. Creative vs. 72. Unimaginative

The Liability of Being Unimaginative: An unimaginative professional fundamentally lacks originality and creativity, severely limiting their capacity to conceptualize new or progressive ideas. This lack of vision stifles creativity and problem-solving, causing people to adhere to routine or outdated approaches, even when they are no longer effective. As a result, these individuals perceive it as challenging to see other options, which limits their ability to plan for the future and its opportunities. Not having creative thinking can slow down progress, cause things to become stuck, and eventually make it harder for an organization to adjust and thrive in a changing world.

The Asset of Being Creative: A creative professional demonstrates extraordinary resourcefulness and a talent for thinking beyond conventional boundaries, generating new ideas and devising clever solutions. They face challenges with fresh perspectives, continually seeking to refine their methods and improve outcomes with innovative ideas. This ability to think creatively not only drives progress forward and enhances how organizations function, but it also enables them to adjust quickly to changing work environments. Being productive and thinking creatively is vital for your professional standing.

The Journey From Unimaginative to Creative: Transitioning from a person who struggles with imagination to a creative thinker requires time and deliberate effort to cultivate an openness to new solutions. It begins with recognizing the limitations of a fixed mindset and actively seeking different concepts, experiences, and perspectives that may challenge our deeply held convictions. They can also experiment with various strategies to handle assignments and overcome difficulties. Your creativity can be significantly enhanced, and new ideas can be generated through curiosity. We also learn new skills, and engage in mentally stimulating activities such as reading widely or exploring various social media resources.

33. Adaptable vs. 73. Inflexible

The Liability of Being Inflexible: An inflexible professional tends to hold firmly to their methods and resists changing their mind, even when there are valid reasons. This can really slow down progress and make it challenging to work together effectively. This rigidity often manifests as a reluctance to identify common ground, a hesitancy to embrace fresh concepts, and a tendency to disregard alternative viewpoints, ultimately impeding creativity and the ability to tackle challenges. When individuals cling too strongly to outdated methods and resist change, they can obstruct progress, making it challenging for teams and organizations to address challenges or seize new opportunities.

The Asset of Being Adaptable: An adaptable professional can easily adapt to new situations and changing circumstances, demonstrating a willingness to change their approach when needed. They embrace challenges and readily adapt to new requirements, which significantly increases their value in a dynamic work environment. This adaptability enables quick responses to unforeseen issues and fosters a more proactive and resilient approach to work. Being open-minded and willing to adapt enables professionals to handle challenges more effectively and produce innovative solutions. They maintain strong relationships at work, making them essential team members in any group effort.

The Transition from Inflexible to Adaptable: Becoming more adaptable involves a significant journey that requires developing self-awareness and a commitment to personal growth. It begins with recognizing how inflexibility can lead to adverse outcomes. These are missed opportunities, stifled creativity, and strained relationships. These issues stem from a reluctance to embrace new ideas and perspectives. This change requires you to pay close attention to listening and to understand different viewpoints, even if they conflict with your existing beliefs. When a person is willing to accept feedback and is open to compromise, they can slowly release their stubbornness and become more flexible. This change enables people to work together more effectively and solve problems more efficiently, ultimately allowing them to develop into more skilled and well-rounded professionals.

34. Focused vs. 74. Procrastinate

The Liability of Being Procrastinate: Procrastination is a professional's worst enemy, turning important tasks into sources of stress by habitually pushing them off until the last possible moment. This isn't just about a minor delay; it means assignments that are perceived as unpleasant or dull get postponed, often until deadlines are practically breathing down your neck. The result? Last-minute scrambling frequently leads to rushed work that's likely to be of lower quality and results in a mounting pile of stress. It can strain relationships with colleagues who depend on your timely input and erode the trust others place in you, making it difficult to be seen as reliable. Ultimately, this habit of deferring action can seriously sabotage your productivity and professional reputation.

The Asset of Being Focused: Conversely, maintaining focus is a valuable professional advantage. It means you can concentrate intensely on your work, giving it the care and precision it deserves, and stay absorbed in tasks until they're completed. You're persistent, constantly working towards objectives and actively minimizing distractions, which is absolutely key for tackling complex projects and delivering truly high-quality outcomes. This unwavering attention ensures your work is done efficiently and significantly reduces the likelihood of making careless errors. Focused professionals are considered productive and reliable, making their contributions invaluable to the success of any team.

The Transition From Procrastinate to Focused: The journey from being a procrastinator to becoming a truly focused individual is a transformative process that requires conscious effort and strategic practice. It usually begins when someone recognizes how much procrastination is costing them and decides to make a genuine change. The results are missed opportunities, increased stress, and a damaged reputation. A key step towards focus involves breaking down overwhelming tasks into smaller, manageable steps, making them feel less daunting and easier to start. Implementing techniques such as time blocking, setting specific and achievable goals for each work session, and creating a dedicated workspace free from distractions are also crucial. By actively practicing single-tasking, celebrating small wins, and establishing a routine that prioritizes diligent work over procrastination, one can gradually retrain one's mind to be consistently focused and productive.

35. Generous vs. 75. Greedy

The Liability of Being Greedy: A selfish professional is overly concerned with their own benefits, like money, power, or fame, frequently disregarding the needs and welfare of others. This trait can manifest as being hesitant to share resources, holding back information, and not genuinely caring about what colleagues need. This leads to a workplace that feels unsupportive. Such self-serving behavior frequently leads to unethical practices, hinders collaboration, and results in a significant decline in team morale. Greedy individuals can damage professional relationships and ultimately undermine the trust and reputation of the company. They prioritized personal accumulation over collective success and demonstrated a covetous, insatiable need for more.

The Asset of Being Generous: A generous professional always goes above and beyond by sharing resources, time, and knowledge. They make positive contributions to the team and help create a supportive and collaborative work environment. They are generous, giving, and supportive, often contributing significantly to help achieve team goals or support their coworkers. They frequently go the extra mile to assist others. Generosity fosters teamwork and morale, demonstrating a commitment to the collective benefit that holds significant value in any professional setting.

The Journey From Greedy to Generous: The focus is on transforming our mindset, shifting from a self-centered perspective to one that recognizes the advantages of collaboration, which benefits all and fosters collective success. Self-awareness is the first step towards bringing about this change. Understanding how greed can negatively impact relationships, trust, and teamwork is crucial. It is also vital to recognize how greed can foster sentiments of alienation and detachment. Actively practicing empathy is a necessary next step. This means making a real effort to understand and appreciate what others need and contribute, which helps to balance out the urge to focus solely on our own interests by actively participating in sharing, whether it be knowledge, time, or resources. And by celebrating the achievements of others as if they were your own. A person can gradually develop a more generous attitude.

36. Just vs. 76. Unjust

The Liability of Being Unjust: Someone who is unjust often acts without regard for fairness or what's right. This could imply that they unfairly favor specific individuals while ignoring others, or they may manipulate rules to benefit themselves. Because they are unable to depend on equitable treatment, this creates an atmosphere in which people lack respect and feel unsafe. Decisions may seem random or influenced by personal preferences, rather than being based on ability or established criteria. The absence of fairness leads to distrust, lowers morale, and obstructs teamwork and the motivation to perform at an optimal level. Ultimately, acting unfairly can harm relationships and foster a toxic environment in the workplace.

The Asset of Being Just: A just person is someone who constantly aims to be fair and shows respect to everyone they encounter. They hold the view that standards should be applied consistently, making choices based on what is fair and proper, rather than on personal bias or self-interest. This dedication to justice and fairness creates a solid base of trust. When individuals are aware that they will be treated justly, they experience a greater sense of security, appreciation, and a drive to put forth their best efforts. A just person creates an environment where everyone feels at ease working together, is encouraged to give their best effort, and can confidently strive towards shared objectives.

The Journey From Unjust to Just: Moving from a situation of injustice to one of justice is a significant change in both our personal lives and our work environments. It usually begins when someone realizes how their choices or actions affect the people around them. Also, when they start to consider what justice truly means in their relationships with others. Being self-aware is the essential first step. The next step is to actively work on changing your approach. Instead of just choosing the option that is most convenient for you, consider what is just for everyone. This requires you to carefully consider other viewpoints and understand how your choices impact others. Furthermore, choose justice even if it may be the more challenging course of action.

37. Optimistic vs. 77. Pessimistic

The Liability of Being Pessimistic: A pessimistic professional consistently views potential problems and adverse outcomes as obstacles, rather than opportunities. This mindset can create a hostile and unproductive environment, viewing obstacles as impossible challenges instead of chances for growth and improvement. When people focus too much on potential failures and become overly preoccupied with challenges, it can significantly hinder creativity, make them hesitant to take risks, and slow down the team's progress. This ongoing negativity not only saps morale and fosters a gloomy work atmosphere but also hinders colleagues from feeling motivated or self-assured. This reality could result in lower productivity and a hesitance to embrace new initiatives.

The Asset of Being Optimistic: An optimistic professional brings a vital sense of hopefulness and assurance to the workplace, maintaining a positive perspective even in the face of challenges. They view challenges as temporary hurdles and opportunities for growth, which fosters resilience in both themselves and their teams. This new method creates a supportive and motivating atmosphere, allowing team members to tackle challenging tasks with confidence and achieve positive outcomes. Focusing on solutions and positive outcomes boosts team spirit, raises productivity, and improves the ability to face challenges.

The Journey from Pessimistic to Optimistic: A person often begins to understand how their negative attitude affects not only themselves but also the people around them, recognizing that it can hinder progress and damage relationships. The following key step is to question and challenge those deeply ingrained negative thoughts actively. Instead of thinking, 'what if it goes wrong?' try replacing it with 'what if it goes right?' or 'what knowledge can I gain from this?' This process involves identifying the positive aspects, acknowledging and valuing minor accomplishments, and cultivating a practice of gratitude for the positive elements in life. All of these activities foster a more robust mindset. Holding onto the conviction that positive outcomes are achievable. This shift may influence how individuals approach their work and enhance their self-assurance when facing challenges.

38. Persuasive vs. 68. Dissuasive:

The Liability of Being Dissuasive: A dissuasive professional typically tries to steer others away from productive paths, often by highlighting potential issues, offering critical feedback, or expressing skepticism about new concepts. This can lead to a gloomy or unsupportive atmosphere, where confidence is lowered and hope for success diminishes. By highlighting difficulties or showing disapproval, they actively work to prevent actions or initiatives, which can stifle creativity and innovation within the team. This habit of dampening enthusiasm can significantly impact team morale, making it more challenging for everyone to pursue ambitious goals. This, in turn, can create challenges in fostering a positive and productive work environment.

The Asset of Being Persuasive: A persuasive communicator knows how to sway others to see things their way or act by using convincing language and trustworthy influence. They possess a remarkable talent for influencing opinions and building consensus by expressing ideas clearly and persuasively, which makes them essential contributors in leadership, sales, or any position that requires support. By clearly sharing their vision and motivating others to act, they bring teams and stakeholders together to work towards shared goals, promoting better collaboration and achieving success. This ability is essential for advancing projects and fostering an environment that encourages collaboration and teamwork.

The Journey From Dissuasive to Persuasive: Shifting from feeling discouraged to feeling inspired requires a significant shift in our behavior. Rather than alienating others, we should concentrate on uplifting them and achieving favorable results. A professional may begin to realize how their negative attitude can harm team spirit, creativity, and overall productivity. The next stage is to actively work on improving communication skills, learning how to articulate thoughts clearly and confidently while concentrating on opportunities and solutions rather than just the issues. You can transform your role from a negative to a positive one by consciously choosing to support and encourage various activities. This fosters trust and motivates your teammates to collaborate and achieve common objectives.

39. Prudent vs. 79. Wasteful

The Liability of Being Wasteful: A wasteful professional frequently handles resources—whether money, time, or materials—in a manner that disregards their lasting value and significance. This habit of being profligate or reckless with resources can significantly harm productivity and sustainability, resulting in less efficient and more expensive operations. This conduct is characterized by disregard for environmental concerns, misappropriation of corporate resources, or noncompliance with budgetary requirements. The situation directly affects profits and has the potential to harm the organization's reputation. Because they are unable to make efficient use of precious assets, misusing resources and opportunities can impede growth for both individuals and teams.

The Asset of Being Prudent: Being prudent is an essential skill in the workplace. It means handling things like time, money, and material resources wisely and thoughtfully. These individuals demonstrate exceptional practical judgment and insight, enabling them to make informed choices that ensure future success and sustainability. This careful approach to distributing resources is crucial for successful long-term planning and ensuring that projects and budgets stay on track. Ultimately, being cautious enables professionals to mitigate risks and enhance outcomes in all their endeavors, thereby making them dependable and valuable team members.

The Journey From Wasteful to Prudent: Shifting from being wasteful to being prudent means transitioning from spending without thought and without planning to managing resources wisely and planning strategically. It usually starts with noticing the real downsides of being wasteful—such as lower efficiency, financial problems, debt, and a damaged reputation. One realizes that these issues stem from not thinking things through carefully. The next step is to work on being more disciplined with how we use our resources, making thoughtful decisions to appreciate and save time, money, and materials. This journey requires us to learn how to make informed choices by considering our long-term needs and interests. It is vital to prioritize decisions that contribute to lasting stability instead of seeking short-term pleasure.

40. Wise vs. 80. Foolish

The Liability of Being Foolish: When someone acts foolishly, they often lack the good judgment or common sense necessary to make informed decisions. This can lead to reckless behavior, a poor ability to plan, or a tendency to ignore the potential consequences of their actions. It can almost always result in adverse outcomes. This lack of foresight can seriously harm their credibility and damage their reputation. Unfortunately, it can lead to costly mistakes that disrupt not only their own work but also the efforts of their entire team. Their choices frequently reflect poor judgment, potentially harming their success and causing unnecessary confusion in the workplace.

The Asset of Being Wise: A wise professional is a vital resource, using their knowledge and insights to make sound decisions and create realistic, practical plans. They possess a strong ability to understand and analyze situations, which enables them to predict possible outcomes. This clear understanding is essential for organizing and successfully addressing even the most challenging tasks. In the end, wisdom acts like a dependable guide, helping professionals determine the best and most advantageous paths in everything they do.

The Journey From Foolish to Wise: The journey from foolishness to gaining wisdom usually begins when a person realizes how their bad decisions and hasty actions have affected not only their own career but also the people around them. The following key step is to enhance your decision-making abilities consciously. This involves seeking knowledge, learning from past mistakes, and genuinely paying attention to the experiences and insights of others. Rather than acting without thinking, a person begins to engage in careful consideration, thoughtful deliberation, and strategic planning. They are constantly weighing the potential outcomes before acting. By using good judgment, learning from each experience, and making informed decisions, people can gradually develop the understanding necessary to manage their careers more effectively and with greater insight.

In Conclusion

Your legacy is not just a statue you create when you stop working; it's a lasting impact that endures long after you're gone. You shape your legacy with every choice you make today. The Becoming pillar encourages you to design that structure yourself. Your character traits—like courage, wisdom, optimism, and vision—are the tools you need to create something meaningful. A leader with these traits does not just handle today; they also prepare for tomorrow. They make a brighter future. They build trust and foster loyalty that extends beyond their position.

If you ignore the value of Becoming, you are building on weak ground. Fear, cynicism, and impaired judgment are not just traits; they are also symptoms of a deeper issue. They actively eat away at us. They create a legacy of missed chances and lost potential. A career that could have stood out fades into nothing. Not making a choice leads to a mediocre outcome. If you fail to plan, the future will surprise you. The result is a reputation that shrinks instead of grows, and an impact that could have been profound remains a faint echo.

The tension between who you are and who you could be shapes your future. It requires you to consciously cultivate the assets that make you resilient, innovative, and essential. The question was never *if* you would leave a legacy, but what kind it would be.

Will it be a story of caution or a testament to courage? Is it a story of being stuck? Or is it a plan for moving forward? Be the author of a story that matters. Choose to build a legacy that could change the world for good.

Vince Gill

"When all is said and one, the only thing you'll have left is your character."

CHAPTER 10

Your Character OS Tune-Up Manual: Live the Life!

Helen Keller

"Character cannot be developed in ease and quiet. Only through experience of trial and suffering can the soul be strengthened, ambition inspired, and success achieved."

Have you ever worked tirelessly for something big? Perhaps you dedicated months to preparing for a major event, invested a year in initiating a significant project at work, or ultimately completed a room renovation in your home. Remember that feeling right after? The rush of accomplishment, the pride, the sheer relief that the most challenging part is over. It's magnificent. But then, a quiet question starts to creep in: *Now what?* The marathon is run, but you still have to get up and go for a jog tomorrow to stay in shape. The project is launched, but now it needs to be managed, updated, and supported. That's where the real, lasting work begins.

My friend, that's precisely where you are right now. You've already made significant progress. You looked at a life that might have been running on autopilot and made the courageous choice to say, "No more." You dove deep into the architecture of your identity, armed yourself with the tools for genuine change, and successfully launched your Character OS Reboot. The fireworks have gone off, and the energy of that initial transformation was, without a doubt, spectacular. But the real magic—the kind that defines who you become and the legacy you leave—unfolds in the quiet, unglamorous moments that follow. It happens on a stressful Tuesday afternoon when your old programming comes knocking at the door, whispering temptations in your ear.

So, let's sit down together, maybe over a virtual cup of coffee, and get real. This next-to-final chapter isn't a conclusion; it's the opposite. It's your official **Character OS Tune-Up Manual**, a lifelong companion for the journey ahead. Think of it this way: you wouldn't buy a lovely car, appreciate its design, and then neglect the oil changes or forget to check the tires. Your character is the most sophisticated, meaningful, and powerful operating system you will ever run, and it deserves at least as much care and attention. The reboot served as the crucial starting point, but true and lasting change occurs through the ongoing, deliberate efforts that come afterward. We are moving away from thinking of this as just a one-time event. Instead, we want it to become a lifelong rhythm, ensuring that the fantastic work you've accomplished remains with you forever. This is the beginning of a lifelong journey where you will explore your creativity and work hard to shape your character into something truly remarkable.

Why Maintenance is Important

From Starting Over to Keeping Things Going

The first thrill of change can be powerful, but it doesn't last forever. Psychologists and behavioral scientists discuss something known as "reversion to the mean." This signifies that, over time, things usually return to their average state. If we do not have a maintenance plan, even our best intentions can gradually disappear. The new habits seem awkward, while the old ones are familiar and cozy. Before we realize it, we find ourselves falling back into the same routines we tried so hard to break. This is the single primary threat to your Character OS: a gradual, almost unnoticeable corruption that builds up over time. It's rarely a big, dramatic failure that throws us off course; it's a slow drift we don't even realize is happening until we're miles from where we wanted to be.

This gradual corruption operates much like a computer virus. This persistent threat can be explicitly identified as EgoOS attempting to reassert control. A small, unchecked habit of impatience or cynicism can act as this "character virus," allowing EgoOS fear- and comparison-based scripts to attach to your new assets and corrupt your system from the inside out. This manual, therefore, is your personal antivirus software. It reframes the "tune-up" not as general maintenance but as a necessary protocol designed to detect, prevent, and neutralize these persistent threats from EgoOS, ensuring your upgraded Character OS remains the dominant program. An antivirus offers real-time protection by scanning for known threats and taking action to eliminate them; similarly, the maintenance routines in this chapter are designed to help you proactively monitor for the return of old liabilities and neutralize them before they can compromise the integrity of your entire Character OS.

This is why we must think of character maintenance not as a chore, but as an art. Imagine your character is a garden you've just beautifully landscaped. The reboot involved removing all the weeds, tilling the soil, and planting seeds for the 40 character assets we had discussed. It looks incredible. But what happens if you walk away? Weeds—those old character liabilities—will inevitably creep back in. Your current aim is to become an expert gardener, nurturing this inner space with thoughtfulness and dedication. You must water the flowers, nourish the soil, and pull weeds as soon as they appear. Regularly taking care of your garden is what helps it not just survive but also thrive beautifully, year after year.

In the center of this garden is your Character Database, a detailed and vibrant collection of your beliefs, values, emotional patterns, and habits. Because of your reboot, it's now packed with substantial resources. This database is not just a locked box or something you can only look at. Your everyday experiences continue to add to this lively, evolving thing we call life. Without a maintenance plan, old bugs and outdated software can resurface, causing your system to slow down or even crash. If we could return to the original concept of this book—a rebooted OS—beware of viruses. Viruses can remain dormant and cause significant damage.

The ultimate goal of this maintenance is to move from *conscious effort* to *unconscious competence*. Do you recall the experience of learning how to drive a car? At first, every movement seemed purposeful, and it was a bit awkward. It was essential to pay attention to the gas pedal, the brake, the steering wheel, and the mirrors while driving. It was exhausting. But with practice, it became second nature. You no longer think about each step; you drive. This is our goal when it comes to character. When you consistently work on your new habits—such as being patient, honest, responsible, and passionate—they start to feel like a natural part of your identity. They become your default response, your typical way of reacting. I call these your default "character convictions."

The Engine of Growth

Getting to Know the Database-Praxis Loop

What actions should we take to make this happen? How can we maintain the garden's beauty while ensuring the engine runs smoothly? How can we neutralize or remove the virus? The power source for your lifelong tune-up is a concept we've touched on, but now we're going to master it: the **Database-Praxis Loop**. This isn't just a fancy theory; it's your personal, practical model for self-diagnosis and self-correction. Let's dissect this engine in detail to make it a tool you can utilize, if not daily, when a virus strikes.

1. **Your Character Database:** Like we discussed earlier, this is your internal operating code repository. Your character is comprised of

everything that defines you: your core values, such as upholding integrity; your beliefs, including viewing failure as an opportunity to learn; your emotional responses, like remaining calm and focused in stressful situations; and your habits, like listening attentively without interrupting others. When you rebooted, you intentionally set up this "new" database with the assets that make you who you are.

2. **Character Praxis-Loop:** "Praxis" is a powerful word. It doesn't just mean "action." It implies an action that is tested in the real world and is followed by reflection. It's where your internal database meets external reality. Every single thing you do—every conversation you have, every decision you make, every deadline you meet—is an act of praxis. It is a live diagnostic test of the code running in your database.

3. **The Loop in Action:** The real magic occurs when these two parts come together in an ongoing cycle. It appears like this:

   - **The Test:** You walk into a meeting where a colleague publicly criticizes your work. This is a moment of praxis. The current situation is actively testing the code stored in your Character Database. What code will run? Will it be the same old glitchy software filled with defensiveness and anger? Or will it be your newly installed program for "grace under pressure" and "seeking to understand"?

   - **The Action:** You take a moment to think and then respond. Imagine that your previous tendency was to react with anger. However, this time, as you utilize your new operating system and you take a moment to pause and express your gratitude by saying, "Thank you for that feedback." I want to make sure I understand everything you're saying. Could you please share more specific details about the observations that are raising concerns?

- **The Reflection & Tune-Up:** As the day goes on, you discover yourself thinking back on the conversation you had. This part of the loop is the most important one. You discover yourself wondering: What was that experience like? Did my response match up with the kind of person I aspire to be? When you recognize that you completed the "patience" program successfully, you help strengthen its neural pathway. This makes it more likely to activate on its own the next time you need it. This reflection serves as a necessary tune-up. You are consciously adjusting and strengthening the code. If you had slipped up and reacted defensively, the reflection would be just as critical. You would diagnose the issue (*"My fear of looking incompetent got triggered"*) and create a corrective plan for the next time (*"When I feel that fear, I will use my 'pause and ask a question' technique"*).

The Database-Praxis Loop serves as the driving force behind all sustainable progress. Character development shifts from being a simple checklist to becoming a lively and engaging dialogue that connects your inner thoughts with your outward behaviors. Every day presents an opportunity to test, improve, and strengthen your Character OS, ensuring it continues to develop and become more resilient over time.

Your Tune-Up Toolkit

The Monthly Pillar Review

To make the Database-Praxis a regular habit, it is essential to establish a structured routine. An engine is no good if you never turn it on. That's where your tune-up toolkit comes in: a periodic, deep-dive review of the **Four Pillars of Character**—Being, Feeling, Doing, and Becoming. Imagine it as a thorough check-up for your inner self, akin to a quarterly review of your character.

This monthly pillar review is entirely optional. It is reserved for chronic character issues that require a deeper resolution. For many who read this book, the Database-Praxis Loop is sufficient to keep your database healthy and strong. You may discover that you have persistent and nagging liabilities in one or two pillars that need "extraction." I believe the monthly pillar review will accomplish the character reset you seek.

How about we try a straightforward rotating schedule? We can concentrate on one pillar each month. This allows each area to receive the attention it needs while the others continue to run in the background. This review process will become routine after a few four-month cycles.

Month 1

The "Being" Tune-Up: Your Core Identity

This month focuses on strengthening your core. You're getting back to the foundation of who you are. It is a way to renew what is most important to you.

- **Key Questions:** "Who am I at my very core, when no one else is watching?" "What are the values that I absolutely cannot compromise on, and did my actions over the past month truly reflect those values?" "Is the story I tell myself about who I am empowering me or holding me back?" "Could any misalignment have slipped in, transforming a strength like 'principled' into a drawback like 'unprincipled'?"
- **Tune-Up Activities:**
    - **Value Journaling:** Every week, pick one of your core values, like integrity, compassion, or discipline. Think

about how you lived it out or where you might not have met that standard.
- **Review:** What is the Character Chart showing you? Is there progress towards the top and right of the chart?
- **Quiet Reflection:** Take 5 minutes to enjoy some quiet time alone. Take this time to really connect with yourself and listen closely to what your inner voice is telling you.

Month 2

The "Feeling" Tune-Up: Understanding Your Emotional Climate

Let's focus on where your emotions feel most at home. Your feelings drive what you do, and being able to control them is a remarkable skill.

- **Key Questions:** This month, how have I typically reacted emotionally to stress, failure, or frustration? "Am I actively deciding how I feel, or am I just slipping back into my old habits and reactions?" "Do I still become angry quickly, or have I learned to take that important moment to pause and breathe before reacting?"
- **Activities for a Tune-Up:**
  - **Emotional Log:** Over the course of one week, keep a record of how you feel and your emotional reactions. Notice what triggers you, how you feel, the physical sensations you have, and how you respond. Pay attention to the patterns that emerge.
  - **Take a moment to pause and reflect.** Take a moment to pause before responding to emails, comments, or requests. This small step can really help you think things through more clearly.

- **Change the way a story is told.** Consider a recurring negative feeling, such as feeling anxious before giving a presentation. Take a moment to jot down a new story that empowers you and boosts your confidence regarding that situation.

Month 3

The "Doing" Tune-Up: A Focus on Your Habits and Actions

This is the moment when your character starts to show themselves to everyone around them. The things you do are a clear reflection of who you are and how you feel about yourself.

- **Important Questions:** "Do my daily habits and routines help me become the person I aspire to be?" "Where is there a gap between what I *say* I believe and what I actually *do?*" "Are my skills, such as active listening, providing constructive feedback, or managing my time, sharp and effective?
- **Tune-Up Activities:**
  - **Habit Check:** Write down the critical habits you do every day. Label each one as either bringing you closer to your goals (+) or taking you further away from them (-). Choose one "-" to substitute.
  - **Integrity Checkpoints:** Set aside some brief moments to ask yourself, "Are my actions in line with my values?"
  - **Skill Practice:** Set aside 5 minutes each day to focus on improving one crucial professional skill. In meetings, try to concentrate on really listening instead of thinking about what you want to say next.

Month 4

The "Becoming" Tune-Up: Your Guiding Light

At last, you step back and reconnect with your goals. Your "Becoming" pillar is what motivates you, the reason behind how you tackle your daily challenges.

- **Key Questions:** "Am I still clear about what I want for my future self in one, five, or ten years? Is it still exciting and motivating?" "In what ways are my actions today helping me become the person I want to be?" "Am I letting distractions or quick thoughts mess with my vision?"
- **Tune-Up Activities:**
    - **Vision Refresh:** Spend a half-hour lunch with your character journal or a writing pad. Dream without limits about your future self.
    - **Write a Letter from Your Future Self:** Picture yourself ten years into the future. Write a letter to yourself, offering advice, encouragement, and perspective.
    - **Find a mentor:** Connect with someone who embodies the qualities you want to develop and reach out to have a conversation.

Your Masterpiece is Complete

An Adventure of Meaningful Development

As we conclude the review of the tune-up manual, I invite you to pause and contemplate the overall picture of your life. It's not vacant nor open-ended. Your life is filled with exciting experiences, shaped by what you have learned and inspired by your dreams. Your Character OS reboot happened when you chose to take charge of your narrative. You decided to grab the brush and take control, becoming the creator of your own story. You addressed the character virus that led to your professional demise and added an ongoing antivirus remedy.

This is a work of art that you never quite complete, and that is what makes it exquisite. It's a work you return to every single day, adding a new stroke of courage here, a touch of humility there, and a vibrant wash of resilience after a professional storm. The process of developing your character happens mostly in private, in the quiet of your heart and mind, but its results are on full public display. You create trust, motivate teams, and lead with honesty.

Keep in mind that this effort has a ripple effect that extends far beyond what you might notice. Your dedication to upholding high character is a testament to your ongoing and ethical leadership. Taking responsibility instead of assigning blame encourages a sense of obligation within your team. Choosing integrity instead of taking shortcuts shows everyone around you just how vital character really is. You are not just growing in isolation; your transformation helps to elevate everyone around you.

There will be setbacks. You will mess up. Old habits will resurface during times of stress. A character virus will attack. Please be patient with yourself. See these moments not as failures, but as crucial system tests—invaluable opportunities to run another diagnostic, to learn, and to strengthen your approach.

Here's my last challenge for you. Think of this Tune-Up Manual as a friend you will have for life. Schedule those pillar reviews in your calendar and protect that time fiercely. Find your character community—the friends and mentors who will hold you accountable and cheer you on.

The palette is set. The brushes are in your hand. Your future is a canvas waiting for your mark. This is your masterpiece to create, your story to tell.

Your character is your most incredible creation—the most important, most beautiful gift you have to give the world.

Pick up the brush. Choose your colors with purpose. And paint. The world truly needs the fantastic person you are right now and the incredible individual you are becoming.

Theodore Roosevelt

"I care not what others think of what I do, but I care very much about what I think of what I do! That is character!"

Key Takeaways

1. Change is an ongoing process, not a one-time event. A significant "reboot" of your life is only the start; real change comes from the steady, everyday actions that come after. Real change takes continuous effort; it's not just about a one-time solution.

2. Regular tune-ups are vital to prevent backsliding. It's natural to drift back to old habits over time slowly. Scheduled maintenance is crucial in counteracting this tendency and ensuring the positive changes you've made are permanent.

3. A structured four-month cycle keeps your growth balanced. Use the provided "Tune-Up Toolkit" to focus on one of the four pillars of character—Being, Feeling, Doing, and Becoming—each month. This helps establish a steady and achievable routine for personal growth.

4. Ask specific questions to help steer your advancement. Every month, we focus on particular questions, such as whether your actions align with your core values or reviewing your daily habits. Regularly checking in with yourself keeps you on track.

5. Personal growth benefits everyone around you. Improving your character is not selfish; it creates a positive ripple effect for your family, team, and community. View setbacks as learning opportunities because true strength is shown by rising after you fall.

CHAPTER 11

Your Game is the Long Game

Aristotle

"We are what we repeatedly do. Excellence, then, is not an act, but a habit."

Your Character OS Is Live

A Concluding Guide to Playing—and Winning—The Long Game

Great job! You have really put in the effort, and it shows! You have successfully gone through the complex journey of restarting your internal "Character OS," and now you are prepared for the next steps ahead. Let's face it, you probably grabbed this guide because you felt really stuck. You were the standout worker, putting in countless hours. You were the committed professional who kept pushing forward, only to see others speed ahead toward their next big opportunity. It was genuinely frustrating. You possessed the skills, the determination, and the ambition, yet it felt like there was an unseen barrier keeping you from moving forward. You developed a profound understanding that the barrier you faced was not something outside of you; it was part of your own internal system. Your character's essential traits—such as discipline, integrity, courage, and accountability—needed a significant enhancement.

We've taken that old system apart, focusing on its essential components, and then rebuilt it from the ground up. This is not just a quick fix; it is a complete redesign based on the Four Pillars of a strong character. This new system is designed to address the challenges we encounter today while also fostering a journey of growth and success throughout our lives. As you transition from the reboot stage to the ongoing "tune-up" phase, it is essential to remember these key elements to ensure your new system operates smoothly. Ultimately, even the most sophisticated software needs regular upkeep to operate at its best. This chapter serves as your roadmap for maintenance—the guide to playing the long game and making sure your journey is filled with unstoppable momentum and genuine fulfillment.

Playing the long game in your career requires understanding that threats to your Character OS are not static; they are constantly evolving. This challenge bears resemblance to cybersecurity, as new and increasingly advanced computer viruses are continually being developed. A computer virus is a type of malware that attaches to programs, replicates itself, and spreads, leading to continuous damage to system performance and data integrity. In the same way, over a long career, you will inevitably encounter new threats. These are not random challenges but the persistent scripts of EgoOS attempting to reassert control through subtle temptations, shifting workplace ethics, or the creeping return of old habits. Therefore, your personal antivirus, as discussed in the previous chapter, cannot be a one-time installation; it must be a subscription that you consciously renew. An antivirus program requires constant updates to its definition files to recognize and eliminate new malware. Similarly, your maintenance protocol must be continuous to detect and neutralize the evolving threat of EgoOS. Also, winning the long game means committing to a lifetime of "updating your defenses" by continuously scanning for these emerging threats and neutralizing them. This ensures your Character OS remains secure and runs at peak performance for decades to come.

Part 1: Your Improved Architecture—A Review of the Four Pillars

Your new Character OS runs on a simple but robust framework. Knowing and frequently reviewing these Four Pillars is the most essential step to making sure your upgrade lasts. As we close this deal, one more succinct review of the four pillars is instructive.

- **Pillar 1: Being.** This is the essence of who you are; it's like your own personal constitution. Think of "Being" as the strong base of core values you choose to uphold, such as honesty, perseverance, compassion, or courage. It's not just about the values you think you should have; it's about knowing and adhering to the principles that show your true self. In real life, this means that when you encounter a difficult decision, you should start by seeking guidance from the "Being" pillar. Does this action reflect the person I want to become? This is the source code for all your best decisions.
- **Pillar 2: Feeling.** This pillar represents your emotional intelligence (EI), a vital aspect of a world that values genuine connection. "Feeling" refers to your capacity to comprehend and handle your own emotions, as well as to identify and impact the emotions of others in your environment. Building meaningful connections with others. Listening to understand rather than just responding. Navigating the complexities of social interactions with confidence. These are key components of effective social interaction. Having a strong "Feeling" pillar helps you avoid sending reactive emails when under stress or misinterpreting a colleague's feedback.
- **Pillar 3: Doing.** If "Being" is your constitutional code, "Doing" is the execution of that code in the real world. This foundation is created through the everyday choices that shape how others

see your dependability, honesty, and respect. It is all about following through on your promises and sticking to the timeline you set. It encompasses all aspects, from meeting deadlines to honoring small commitments to colleagues. Every time you keep a promise, you build up the core of who you are. Trust is not built on big promises; it is formed through steady and reliable actions that people can see and count on.

- **Pillar 4: Becoming.** Your vision serves as your benchmark, guiding you through the unpredictable paths of life and your career. In a world that's constantly changing, AI and remote work are reshaping how we engage. Your "Becoming" pillar serves as both your anchor and your guide. It is a vivid and engaging image of the person you are becoming and the influence you aspire to create. This vision fuels your motivation and sharpens your focus. It gives you the strength to tackle short-term challenges, knowing they are just stepping stones on a much larger journey.

Part 2: The Engine of Growth—Understanding the Database-Praxis Cycle

Understanding your core values is one thing; embodying them is a whole different challenge. The main way your new Character OS works is through something we refer to as the "Database-Praxis Loop"—your hidden advantage when facing life's unexpected challenges. Character isn't forged in a single, dramatic lightning-bolt moment; it's built in the small, quiet choices you make every single day. This loop is the journey that transforms good intentions into strong, lasting habits.

Consider it your ability to take a moment and make a thoughtful decision. Here's the deal: you come across a situation, i.e., a passive-aggressive email from a coworker, a project that's unexpectedly gone haywire, or a request that really pushes your limits. Your old operating system would quickly switch to a defensive stance, either sending out a hasty response or shutting down in annoyance. But your new OS has a different protocol.

First, you **pause**. You resist the primal urge to react instantly. You take one, two, three deep breaths. This small gap creates the space needed for positive intentionality. Second, you **consult your internal database**. This is where you access your Four Pillars. You ask yourself: What would a person of integrity do here (Being)? What is the most emotionally intelligent way to handle this (Feeling)? What action would uphold my commitments and align with my reputation (Doing)? What choice moves me closer to the person who leads now and in the future (Becoming)?

Finally, you **choose your action (Praxis)**. Based on the wisdom gained, you reboot and store it in your internal database, and then you select a response. You don't just react; you respond with purpose. Maybe you walk over to your colleague's desk to clarify their email instead of firing back. Perhaps you could calmly bring your team together to evaluate the "urgent" project instead of panicking. Your colleagues will start to notice. They might wonder if you've been secretly replaced by a Zen master who turns tension into teamwork. The answer is yes; you have indeed been replaced. And the master is you.

Part 3: The Maintenance Plan—Three Reminders for the Long Game

Now that your system is live and you're practicing the loop, the final piece is establishing a routine for maintenance. Your character isn't a "set it and forget it" crockpot meal; it's more like a prized, and yes, robust mindset that needs regular attention to thrive. Here are three key principles that will keep you optimistic, inspired, and consistently tuning up your OS for the long game ahead.

1. Embrace Glitches as Comedy Gold, Not Catastrophe

Let's be clear: you will make mistakes. There will be days when stress is high, sleep is low, and you suddenly snap at a coworker or procrastinate on a critical task, channeling your old, glitchy self. At such moments, resist the temptation to declare the entire character reboot a catastrophic failure. Instead, get your inner engineer on and laugh it off like a sitcom blooper. See these moments for what they are: "diagnostic tests." Your system is simply running a check and has found a bug. Get curious, not critical. Run a friendly diagnostic through your four pillars: Was this a failure of Being (I chose convenience over my values)? A failure of Feeling (I was emotionally burnt out and missed the cues)? A failure of Doing (I let a commitment slide)? Or a failure of Becoming (I let fear of the future paralyze me)? Every bug you find and fix is not a setback; it is an opportunity for growth that strengthens your entire system. Even superheroes stumble sometimes. Your ability to bounce back with elegance and a touch of humor is what really sets you apart as legendary.

2. Become the Ripple Effect Champion (No Title Required)

Here is where the journey gets genuinely exciting. Your character upgrade doesn't exist in a vacuum. Whether you asked for it or not, you are now a leader. You don't need a corner office or a fancy title on your business card to have a profound impact. When you operate on your new OS, you become a pebble of awesomeness dropped into the office pond, and the ripples of positive change spread far and wide. Think about it. When you genuinely listen in a meeting, you permit others to speak up. Owning up to a mistake in a public setting with grace helps to foster trust and creates a sense of psychological safety for everyone on your team. When you genuinely celebrate a teammate's success, you push back against negativity and create an environment of support for one another. You are truly transforming the atmosphere around you. This positive energy is hilariously contagious, spilling over into your family life and friendships. Be mindful of this new superpower. Your character is now creating an atmosphere that encourages others to escape their own stagnation, demonstrating that true success comes from maintaining integrity. You are not only creating a career; you are also crafting a legacy filled with kindness and innovation.

3. Cultivate Your Character Like a Productivity Engine

Big, dramatic gestures are not always effective. The real secret to making excellence a permanent part of who you are lies in tiny, consistent habits. You must nurture your character with the same diligence you'd apply to a prized pet or a fussy houseplant. Don't just hope for the best; schedule the care. You can do this by habit-stacking like a productivity ninja, but for your soul.

- **Schedule Weekly Reflections:** Please set aside 10 minutes each Friday to reflect on your week. Where did you nail it? Where did you glitch? Celebrate the wins and analyze the bugs.
- **Book Monthly Pillar Audits:** Treat this like a VIP meeting with yourself. Go through each of the Four Pillars and honestly assess your alignment. This keeps your benchmark in focus.
- **Create Environmental Cues:** Stick a note on your monitor that says, "Be the oak" or "Pause, you magnificent creature!" Occasionally, these little reminders can give you the focus you need when things get tough.

Little things, such as consistent watering and adequate sunlight, transform intentional practice into a natural state. When excellence shifts from being something you strive for to becoming a part of who you are, it transforms into a quiet yet powerful force that fuels your success and brings you true fulfillment.

In Conclusion: Create Your Own Masterpiece

You have started a journey from feeling trapped to believing that nothing can hold you back. Remember that your character is a magnificent canvas, and every single day presents a new opportunity to add fresh brushstrokes of kindness, empathy, resilience, and integrity.

Reading Character OS for Professionals will facilitate a Character OS Reboot for most professionals. A Personal Companion Workbook is available to facilitate implementation and application. Also available is Dr. A's Character Workshop online course for those with stubborn liabilities who need additional assistance to recover lost assets and remove or neutralize persistent liabilities. The QR code at the end of this book will connect you to these extra Character OS Reboot resources, including a monthly newsletter.

Achieving long-term success requires a strong foundation in your identity. You have rebooted your system. You have the tools for the tune-ups. You have the vision for your future. Now inspire the world. This long game? It is absolutely, unequivocally, 100% yours to win. Paint boldly, laugh often, and watch your incredible future unfold.

Benjamín Alicea-Lugo, PhD

"I prioritize values over convenience. I pause before I react. I learn in public and practice in private. I am the oak in the storm—rooted, unshakeable, and constantly growing."

APPENDIX 1

Roots of Character OS: Historical Perspectives and Ancient Wisdom

Jesus Christ from Nazareth

"Teacher, which is the greatest commandment in the Law?" Jesus replied, "Love the Lord your God with all your heart and with all your soul and with all your mind." This is the first and greatest commandment. And the second is like it: 'Love your neighbor as yourself.' All the Law and the Prophets hang on these two commandments." Matthew 22: 36-40

This chapter examines historical perspectives and ancient wisdom. These ideas help shape our understanding of character. It explores the ideas, values, and methods that have shaped character development throughout history and across diverse cultures. Consider it a system scan. It shows the compatibility requirements necessary for rebooting your Character OS. This view helps you lead and grow. You may be familiar with some of these sources of ancient wisdom. For some, it may be a new beginning. For others, it may be a chance to reconnect with valuable lessons from the past.

The Endless Search for Character

The question, "What is good character?" is not just a trend. It is a timeless pursuit. For thousands of years, ancient philosophers and modern self-help experts have tried to define and embody strong character. Why is that? Character is the foundation of a meaningful life.

It helps people find fulfillment, achieve goals, and create social harmony. We naturally recognize its significance.

A quick online search for "character quality list" or "how to build character" shows thousands of results. You will see school curricula, religious teachings, leadership manifestos, psychological blogs, and parenting columns. The amount can be too much to handle.

Imagine a vast, quiet library. Rows of neatly shelved books stretch in every direction. Each one offers a distinct perspective on character development. This variety shows a common concern. It highlights a shared human wish to grow, improve, and live with purpose.

With so many sources, how can you avoid digital overload? Which lists are invaluable? What philosophies provide more than just poetic language? What gives clear, practical steps for real growth?

This chapter guides you through the vast library. We will look at essential figures and traditions. These are both historical and spiritual. They have helped shape our understanding of character. We will examine how their ideas align, where they diverge, and what insights they offer for our journey. Examining these perspectives will provide you with a broader understanding of the character landscape. This will help you make better choices for your ongoing reboot.

A Journey Through Character Frameworks

Significant Contributors and Their Ideas

To understand modern character development, we must examine the key thinkers who have shaped its evolution. Their ideas continue to influence our perspectives on personal development and morality. In this section, we will explore several major perspectives in sequence. This exploration starts with a powerful voice from history. This exploration demonstrates how the discussion about character has evolved and expanded over time.

1. The Secret to a Good Life: Aristotle's "Just Right" Idea

We start with Aristotle, who was a Greek philosopher. He lived from 384 to 322 BC. The Nicomachean Ethics remains relevant today. Think about personal development. It's not like building a house or creating an app. Becoming the best version of yourself is the key. That's the core of Aristotle's question: What does it mean to live well?

His answer was not about fame or fortune. He talked about eudaimonia (you-die-mo-NEE-ah). This term means "flourishing" or "thriving." A healthy plant receives the right amount of sun and water. It grows, it's vibrant, and it's alive. Eudaimonia means living a complete life. It's about reaching your deepest potential.

"Okay," you might wonder, "but how do I get there?"

Aristotle advised building good character habits. These habits form the basis of a fulfilling life. He presented a significant concept known as the Golden Mean. It's like the "Goldilocks Rule": not too much, not too little, but exactly right.

Aristotle says that each virtue lies between two harmful extremes. Let us use courage as an example.

You see your friend getting bullied. You feel scared and do nothing. That is being cowardly.

You rush in without thinking. This makes everything worse and leads to chaos you cannot handle. That is reckless.

You walk over calmly. You support your friend. You tell the bully to stop firmly. You feel scared, but you go for it anyway. Courage is the Golden Mean in action.

This rule applies to nearly everything in life.

Consider generosity, for example.

You take all the pizza for yourself.

Giving too much can leave you empty. You might end up hungry.

You share fairly. This way, everyone gets a slice and enjoys it. That shows generosity.

What is humor?

Not laughing at all? You are bored.

Always joking, never serious? You are funny.

Is it the right balance? You are clever. You know how a good joke can brighten the mood.

How can you be brave, generous, or witty?

Aristotle gives important advice: reading about virtue will not make you virtuous. You need to practice.

Consider how you learn to play basketball. To be a great shooter, you cannot just read the rulebook; you must also practice. You step onto the court and take a shot. You miss it first. Your body learns over time. Your aim gets better. It eventually becomes second nature.

Character functions similarly. Do you want to be brave? Take brave steps, even if they are small. Do not let your racing heart hold you back. Do you want to be generous? Start by giving, even if it is just a little. When you pick the "just right" response, you practice virtue. You are changing your Character OS. Step by step, these actions shape your identity.

Aristotle believes that living well involves dedicating oneself to this lifelong journey. It is not just a goal. It is an ongoing journey. Always aim for balance. Continue to develop habits that make you proud. You will live a life filled with meaning, power, and significance.

2. Religious and Spiritual Traditions: Ancient Blueprints for Moral Character

Religions and spiritual traditions have offered moral guidance for thousands of years. This was long before psychology became a formal discipline. They serve as guides for character development. They shape human behavior and values in diverse cultures and generations.

These traditions provide clear moral guidelines. They share inspirational stories about role models. They provide frameworks for cultivating virtues. They warn against destructive behaviors. They create a keen sense of purpose and meaning.

Character development is closely tied to personal fulfillment and overall well-being. It fosters community harmony and a connection to something sacred, such as divine truth or a higher power.

The Judeo-Christian Heritage

Shaping the Western View of Character.

The Judeo-Christian tradition has significantly influenced Western notions of morality and virtue. It offers a clear model for character growth. This model is based on sacred texts, teachings, and lasting cultural practices.

Judaism

Ethical Directives and Moral Growth

The Hebrew Bible, rabbinic literature, and the Talmud offer essential lessons on ethics and morality within the Jewish tradition. Some important concepts are evident:

- **Middot** are the ethical traits or moral qualities that influence our everyday actions. Developing middot is crucial for Jewish ethics and personal growth.
- **Chesed (Loving-Kindness):** Chesed is more than just an emotion; it involves taking compassionate action. Volunteering at a soup kitchen, providing support to those who are grieving, or helping others without expecting anything in return are all great ways to show kindness.
- **Tzedakah (Justice/Righteousness):** This is more than just charity; it's a responsibility we need to embrace. Giving to others fairly and fighting for social justice reflect a person's true character.
- **Emet (Truth/Integrity)**: Even in demanding situations, integrity demands honesty and moral consistency.
- **Anavah (Humility)**: This is an awareness of one's place in relation to others and to God. It tempers ego and fosters mutual respect.

- **Savlanut (Patience):** The ability to endure hardship and support composure in adversity is considered a key virtue.

Pirkei Avot (Ethics of the Fathers)

This famous part of the Mishnah includes ethical lessons and thoughts from ancient sages. It acts as a moral guide. It helps readers to build strong, purpose-driven character.

Make thoughtful and good choices.

Stay open to learning. Ask yourself, "Who is wise?" A person who learns from everyone.

This attitude encourages humility and ongoing personal development. Wisdom is more than just knowing everything; it is also about understanding and insight. It is about being open to learning from anyone.

The Mussar Movement

The Mussar Movement began in the 1800s in Eastern Europe. It gave a disciplined way for people to grow spiritually and ethically. It focused on daily ethical self-examination. It included a consistent study of moral texts. It also emphasized the deliberate cultivation of virtues like gratitude, honesty, and restraint.

Practitioners engage in exercises such as journaling, reciting affirmations, and tracking their moral successes and failures. The goal was to improve the soul with careful work. This was not just for show. It was about real inner change.

Christianity

A New Covenant for Change Within

Christian character development is based on Jewish moral foundations. It focuses on the life, teachings, and example of Jesus Christ, as shown in the New Testament. It focuses on internal change rather than just outside actions.

Foundational Teachings

From Commandments to Inner Virtues

- **The Ten Commandments are found in Exodus 20 and Deuteronomy 5.** These provide clear moral boundaries. They are guidelines for ethical living. These are still central to Judeo-Christian moral thought.
- **The Sermon on the Mount (Matthew 5–7):** This collection of Jesus' teachings shows the core of Christian ethics. It does not just tell us how to act. It changes our entire inner life to align with the values of the Kingdom of God. The Ten Commandments ban specific actions. The Sermon on the Mount goes further. It looks at motives, attitudes, and virtues.

This sermon focuses on the Beatitudes. They are a series of surprising blessings. They change how we view success, happiness, and spiritual growth. Many scholars view the Sermon on the Mount as the "Constitution" of Christianity.

The Beatitudes (Matthew 5:3-12)

Radical Values of the Kingdom

The Beatitudes go against common beliefs. They do not celebrate the powerful, the wealthy, or the self-important. They honor those who are often overlooked. The humble, the merciful, and the justice-seekers. These are not just passing feelings. They are virtues that reveal a person's true character. They are based on God's values.

"Blessed are those who show mercy, for they will receive compassion."

Mercy is not just feeling sorry for someone. It is about helping them. It means to forgive those who have hurt you. It's about letting go of bitterness. It also involves helping the poor, the sick, or those in grief. Mercy shows God's true nature. It helps heal broken relationships and communities. This creates a cycle of grace that changes both the giver and the receiver.

"Blessed are those with pure hearts, for they will see God."

Purity of heart means being sincere, open, and focused on one goal. A pure-hearted person behaves with integrity. They are honest and straightforward. Their intentions are selfless. Their actions match their beliefs. Being honest and straightforward helps create a strong bond with God. There are no pretenses or barriers involved.

"Blessed are the peacemakers. They will be called children of God."

Peacemaking involves facing conflict directly, rather than avoiding it. It is about confronting it with bravery and understanding. The goal is to bring back harmony. A peacemaker resolves conflicts. They repair damaged relationships and advocate for justice with compassion and understanding. This vital work reflects God's mission of bringing people together. People who take it on are called "children of God." They actively take part in divine healing.

The Call for Change in Character

The Beatitudes and the Sermon on the Mount encourage Christians to embody God's character in their daily lives. Supporting God's Kingdom isn't about big religious shows. It's about making daily choices. Show mercy, pursue purity, and build peace.

Christian character emphasizes growth over mere actions. It means becoming a person who represents kindness, humility, and grace in everyday life.

Pauline Character

The Fruit of the Spirit (Galatians 5:22–23)

In his letter to the Galatians, the Apostle Paul presents a clear vision of a transformed Christian life. He compares two separate ways of living. One is driven by selfish human impulses, which he calls the "works of the flesh." The other is influenced by a strong connection with God's Spirit.

In his letter to the Galatians, the Apostle Paul talks about the "works of the flesh." These are actions that stem from our sinful nature, not from following God. He provides many examples of these behaviors. They include immorality, impurity, and indecency. He mentions idolatry. This means putting anything or anyone above God. He also talks about sorcery. This involves attempting to control or manipulate others using malicious or unethical powers. Paul also discusses hatred, strife, jealousy, anger, and selfish ambition. These negative traits can harm our relationships with others. Envy, drunkenness, and wild parties are other manifestations of the flesh. These can cause chaos and harm. Paul cautions that those who persist in this lifestyle will not enter the kingdom of God. This means they will not have eternal life with Him. Paul urges the Galatians, and us today, to let go of sinful behaviors. He wants us to live by the Spirit. We should follow God's guidance and embrace a life of love, kindness, and self-control.

The Spirit-led life centers on what Paul refers to as "the fruit of the Spirit." Paul uses the word "fruit" instead of "fruits." This distinction demonstrates that these nine virtues form a unified whole. They are a single spiritual harvest. This harvest grows naturally in a person whose heart is consistently nourished by divine presence. These qualities are not just checklists of behaviors or achievements. They come from a renewed inner life. They change emotional well-being and external relationships.

The Internal Core

Love, Joy, and Peace

The first three virtues illustrate the internal transformation that a Spirit-led life brings about. They focus mainly on the heart's attitude toward God, oneself, and the world.

- Love (Agape) is not about romance or friendship. It is selfless, unconditional, and sacrificial. It prioritizes the well-being of others over personal gain. There is no expectation of anything in return. This type of love serves as the foundation for all other spiritual gifts. It shows through forgiveness, service, empathy, and compassion. This includes those we see as adversaries.
- Joy is different from happiness. Happiness changes with outside events. Joy is a lasting feeling. It comes from a strong relationship with God. It exists alongside sorrow, pain, and hardship. It shows itself as an optimistic spirit, unaffected by life's challenges.
- Peace is often referred to as "Shalom." It stands for harmony and tranquility. This term is used in various contexts,

emphasizing the importance of calmness and well-being. Peace is more than just the absence of conflict; it is a state of harmony and tranquility. It means "shalom." This is a feeling of well-being, completeness, and harmony. Inner calm protects the heart from fear and anxiety. It helps us face life with peace and encourages healing in relationships.

Relational virtues include patience, kindness, and goodness.

Three virtues guide our interactions with others. They show what is inside. Love, joy, and peace shape these feelings.

- Forbearance means having patience. It's the ability to handle discomfort, delays, or tough people without getting frustrated or retaliating. It requires tolerance and patience. Emotional maturity is critical to maintaining composure when faced with provocation. This involves allowing others the freedom to develop. It requires attentive listening and responding to difficulties with compassion and empathy.
- Kindness is love in action. Kindness is showing care. It comes from thoughtful words and gentle actions. Being approachable, helpful, and generous is a good habit. Small, everyday actions can show it. A kind person makes others feel safe and trusted. They create a welcoming atmosphere wherever they are.
- Goodness extends beyond kindness. It demonstrates moral integrity by taking appropriate actions. It combines compassion with fairness. A reasonable person acts kindly. They advocate for what is right, even in challenging situations. They emphasize truth, justice, and moral clarity. They are viewed as reliable leaders.

Inner strength comes from faithfulness, gentleness, and self-control.

The last three virtues in Paul's list are faithfulness, gentleness, and self-control. They show the inner strength that helps build a mature character. These qualities form a foundation. They support the visible virtues and help create a balanced, Spirit-led life.

- Faithfulness shows that a person is reliable, trustworthy, and loyal. It means keeping promises. It means honoring commitments. It means being consistent in what you say and do. A faithful person is loyal to God and others. They stay correct and dependable. Trust is key in all relationships. Faithfulness shows a steady and reliable character.
- Gentleness is also known as meekness. People often see gentleness as weakness. But it is a strength that is under control. A gentle person shares their truth and beliefs in a calm and respectful manner. They do not use aggression or arrogance. This quality includes being humble, patient, and respectful in every interaction. It's about correcting others kindly. You can speak assertively without being confrontational. You also handle disagreements with grace.
- Self-control is an important virtue. It means managing your desires, emotions, impulses, and actions. A person with self-control does not let passions or instincts take over. Instead, they show discipline in their thoughts, words, and actions. Self-control helps love stay patient. It lets joy get through tough times. It also helps peace win over anxiety. It connects all the fruits. This way, they consistently appear in daily life.

Virtues and vices are essential in Christian thought. They shape how people live and interact with one another. Virtues are good qualities, such as kindness and honesty. Vices are negative traits, like greed and anger.

Understanding these concepts helps in moral decision-making. They guide believers in their faith and actions.

Christian theology has grown in its understanding of character. Thinkers such as St. Augustine and Thomas Aquinas developed detailed frameworks of virtue. They combined Aristotelian virtue ethics with Christian teachings. This combination created clear guidelines for moral behavior.

- The Four Cardinal Virtues are prudence, justice, fortitude, and temperance. Prudence means wise decision-making. Justice stands for fairness. Fortitude stands for courage. Temperance is about moderation. Temperance guides ethical living and practical wisdom in daily life.
- The three theological virtues are faith, hope, and charity, which is love. These virtues come from a relationship with God. They demonstrate the critical spiritual values we strive for.
- The Seven Deadly Sins are pride, greed, lust, envy, gluttony, wrath, and sloth. These sins represent harmful traits that weaken both character and spiritual well-being.

The Christian journey is not about becoming perfect right away. It is about growing and reflecting Christ's character over a lifetime. Local Christian groups, national denominations, and global faith organizations provide structured teachings. They offer scripture-based insights and ethical resources to support this growth. Sunday school, seminary, Bible study groups, and published devotionals all focus on biblical virtues. They emphasize moral decision-making as a crucial aspect of personal and community development.

A Wider Spiritual Perspective

Worldwide Religious Impacts on Character

Judeo-Christian traditions have greatly influenced Western ideals. However, other major world religions also offer valuable insights into moral growth. Their teachings have influenced civilizations. They continue to provide helpful talks on virtue, ethics, and personal development.

Islam

The Character of the Believer (Akhlaq)

Akhlaq, or character, in Islam is viewed as a clear reflection of faith and a crucial aspect of one's connection with God. The Qur'an and the Sunnah, which reflect the teachings of the Prophet Muhammad, direct Muslims in developing essential virtues.

- Rahmah, or compassion, shows God's merciful nature. It is demonstrated through forgiveness, kindness, and tenderness toward all living beings.
- Sidq (Truthfulness): It goes beyond simply being honest in what we say; sidq requires total sincerity, ensuring that our inner beliefs align with our outward actions. It forms the basis of individual honesty and collective confidence.

Adl (Justice) is a fundamental moral obligation that emphasizes fairness and equity. Believers should stand for justice, even when it conflicts with their own interests, to ensure harmony and protect human dignity.

These values are not just abstract concepts; they are active virtues that form a Muslim's character, fostering trust, mercy, and moral courage.

Buddhism

The Noble Eightfold Path

Through the Noble Eightfold Path, Buddhism provides a straightforward guide for ethical and spiritual living, aiming to alleviate suffering and lead to enlightenment. It includes three key areas:

- Ethical Conduct:
  - Right Speech: Speaking truthfully and kindly
  - Right Action: Behaving ethically and non-violently
  - Right Livelihood: Earning a living without harming others

- Mental Discipline:
  - Right Effort: Cultivating positive thoughts and intentions
  - Right Mindfulness: Being present and aware of thoughts and actions
  - Right Concentration: Practicing focused meditation

- Wisdom:
  - Right Understanding: Seeing reality clearly
  - Right Intention: Aligning motivations with compassion and wisdom

This framework promotes ethical self-awareness, emotional clarity, and compassionate behavior, serving as a practical guide for personal growth, inner peace, and building harmonious relationships with others.

Hinduism

Dharma and Yogic Ethics

Dharma in Hindu philosophy signifies the universal moral order and the personal duties individuals must fulfill to keep harmony in the universe. It forms the foundation for living well, which includes ethical behavior, social responsibility, and alignment with universal principles.

In yogic traditions, especially in Raja Yoga as described in Patanjali's Yoga Sutras, ethical conduct is organized into:

1. Yamas (Ethical Restraints – External Discipline):
   - Ahimsa (Non-violence in thought, word, and action)
   - Satya (truthfulness and integrity)
   - Asteya (Non-stealing; avoiding exploitation)
   - Brahmacharya (Traditionally celibacy, but more broadly, moderation in sensory pursuits)
   - Aparigraha (Non-attachment; freedom from greed)

2. Niyamas (internal observations—personal discipline):
   - Shaucha (Purity of body and mind)
   - Santosha (Contentment and gratitude)
   - Tapas (Discipline, perseverance, and austerity)
   - Svadhyaya (Self-study, scriptural study, and introspection)
   - Ishvarapranidhana (Surrender to a higher consciousness or divine will)

The Yamas and Niyamas are key practices for living a good and yogic life, guiding ethical behavior, personal growth, and spiritual development. They encourage balance in society as well as within the mind and spirit.

Indigenous Spiritual Traditions

Insights Gained from Stories and Connections

Indigenous spiritual traditions worldwide offer intriguing perspectives on a character deeply connected to community, nature, and spirituality. Traditions convey wisdom through stories, rituals, and community events.

Every aspect of life encompasses essential values such as respect, reciprocity, courage, and kinship. Rather than imposing strict rules, these traditions illustrate that character is shaped by living in harmony with others, nature, and the spiritual realm.

These virtues guide individuals to:

- Live in harmony with nature.
- Respect your ancestors and value the knowledge they shared.
- Show bravery and compassion when dealing with difficulties.
- Show respect for everyone, as well as all living creatures and our planet.

A Common Thread

Inner Growth Through Spiritual Practice

Across all primary religious and spiritual paths—whether Hinduism, Buddhism, Islam, Christianity, Judaism, or indigenous beliefs—a shared theme emerges: actual character development begins within.

This internal transformation is not abstract; it is supported through:

- Spiritual disciplines like prayer, meditation, mindfulness, and fasting.
- Examining sacred texts that influence moral thinking and enhance values.

- Mentorship and community promote accountability and act as examples.
- Service to others expresses inner virtue through outward action.

These practices cultivate not just self-improvement but a deep integration of belief, behavior, and belonging.

A Common Thread

Growing Inside Through Spiritual Practice

Although they originate from unusual places and hold unique beliefs, these religious and spiritual traditions share a common thread. They all show that building character is essential for personal growth and finding a meaningful life. Spiritual practice can take many forms. It might be prayer, meditation, or reflecting on ethics. Community rituals and helping others also play a role. All these methods aim to improve and strengthen character. These methods provide timeless guides that remain especially useful for individuals and communities seeking to achieve success.

In Conclusion

This Appendix, "Roots of Character—Historical Perspectives and Ancient Wisdom," looks at key ideas about character development from the past. People have always looked for good character. They see it as essential for success in life and work. We explored old philosophical ideas. We focused on Aristotle's view of living a complete life, known as eudaimonia. He emphasized building good habits by finding the "just right" amount, or Golden Mean, through regular practice. This chapter examines the influence of religion and spiritual traditions on character development. We examined how Judaism, Christianity, Islam, Buddhism, Hinduism, and Indigenous traditions offer various but interconnected ways to live a moral and ethical life. Each tradition has its teachings, such as Middot in Judaism, the Beatitudes in Christianity, Akhlaq in Islam, the Noble Eightfold Path in Buddhism, Dharma in Hinduism, and the values in Indigenous cultures. They emphasized personal growth and community care.

This study shows that, despite diverse backgrounds and beliefs, older philosophies and spiritual traditions share a key idea. Character goes beyond just thoughts in your mind. It is built through steady inner growth. You need to check your morals. Dedicated spiritual or ethical practice is essential. Everyone agrees that understanding the "ecosystem" of character is critical for personal and professional growth. This understanding creates a solid foundation. It helps us navigate challenging situations. It also leads to a life filled with meaning, strength, and significance. Paul recommended that we focus on what is good and worthy of praise. This helps us build a mindset of honesty and purpose. Building character starts from within. This view of history is the essential foundation. It supports innovative ideas and methods for character development.

President Abraham Lincoln

Character is like a tree, and reputation is its shadow. The shadow is what we think it is, and the tree is the real thing.

APPENDIX 2

Modern Character OS Development: From Science to Practical Application

Maya Angelou

"I've learned that people will forget what you said, people will forget what you did, but people will never forget how you made them feel."

Introduction

We will now turn to the contemporary world, having explored the wisdom of ancient spiritual traditions and ideologies that have shaped our understanding of character. This chapter examines how modern ideas, informed by methodical approaches and scientific knowledge, place a strong emphasis on character development and its application in daily life, particularly for individuals working in the public sector.

We will examine individuals like Benjamin Franklin, who employed his "Thirteen Virtues" and meticulous self-reporting to develop a pragmatic, nearly scientific approach to moral development. We will also examine Stephen Covey's essential framework, which emphasizes a focus on the "Character Ethic" based on strong ethical principles, moving beyond superficial "Personality Ethic" traits to develop truly effective habits. These modern methods build on old wisdom and offer clear, practical steps. They highlight the importance of regular and purposeful practice for developing character.

This appendix will highlight how these frameworks offer practical tools for "upgrading your internal operating system" and transforming abstract concepts into tangible actions, aiming for what we call "Character Praxis." As we move from understanding to application, we'll see how various modern models look to provide clear, actionable guidance for developing a robust, resilient, and responsive internal system—a truly effective "Character OS" for navigating the demands of modern life and leadership. The goal is to equip you with the practical solutions needed for a successful personal and professional reboot.

1. Benjamin Franklin (1706–1790): A Practical Route to Ethical Excellence

The statesman, inventor, and author Benjamin Franklin offered a secular yet remarkably organized approach to character formation during the American Enlightenment. Franklin described his aspirational objective of attaining moral perfection in his autobiography, addressing personal development with the vision of a reformer and the discipline of a scientist.

Franklin created the "Thirteen Virtues," a valuable framework for personal development, during his youth. He tracked a different virtue in a small notebook every week, treating his character as if it were an individual experiment. He was not looking for perfection; he aimed to become better by being aware each day and practicing with purpose.

Franklin's Thirteen Virtues: A Life Audit in Action

1. **Temperance—managing** your desires and steering clear of overindulgence.
2. **Silence** – Speak only with purpose or value.

3. **Order** – Let everything have its place and time.
4. **Resolution** – Follow through on goals with determination.
5. **Frugality** – Waste nothing. Use resources wisely.
6. **Industry** – Always be engaged in something worthwhile.
7. **Sincerity** – Be honest and genuine. Stay honest.
8. **Justice**—Act justly and appropriately, even if it is not easy.
9. **Moderation** – Stay balanced; don't respond too strongly or too weakly.
10. **Cleanliness**—Keep your body and surroundings clean.
11. **Tranquility** – Stay calm in the face of chaos or minor misfortunes.
12. **Chastity** – Practice self-respect and mutual respect in intimate matters.
13. **Humility** – Emulate Socrates and Jesus; always be open to learning.

Franklin's method was brilliant and simple: each week, he concentrated on one virtue and noted any mistakes by marking them with black marks in his notebook. He would cycle through all the virtues over 13 weeks, repeating this process four times a year. This self-monitoring method encouraged discipline, self-awareness, and accountability, supporting growth without being judgmental.

Franklin realized that perfection was impossible, but the effort to achieve it led to significant change. His legacy delivers a lasting message: character can be developed—deliberately, systematically, and gradually.

2. VIA Institute on Character: Understanding Strengths (Late 20th Century–Present)

One significant advancement in the field of positive psychology was the VIA Institute on Character, co-founded by Dr. Neal Mayerson, Dr. Martin Seligman and Dr. Christopher Peterson. The Institute developed the VIA Classification of Character Strengths and Virtues—a modern "manual of the sanities" that scientifically categorizes positive human traits found across cultures and periods.

The 24 Character Strengths (Grouped into 6 Core Virtues)

Think of your character as a set of 24 inner strengths—qualities that help you succeed. These strengths are grouped into six core virtues, each representing a distinct aspect of human excellence:

- Wisdom is your ability to think deeply and creatively. Included are creativity, curiosity, judgment, a love of learning, and a broad perspective.
- Courage is your ability to act despite fear or difficulties. Included are bravery, perseverance, honesty, and zest.
- Humanity—your power to form meaningful connections.
- Included: Love, Kindness, and Social Intelligence.
- Justice—Your power to lead, collaborate, and contribute to the common good.
- Included: Teamwork, Fairness, and Leadership.
- Temperance—Your ability to maintain self-control and balance. Included are forgiveness, humility, prudence, and self-regulation.
- Transcendence is your ability to discover purpose and meaning that goes beyond yourself. It contains: Gratitude, Hope, Humor, and Appreciation for Beauty and Excellence.

Importantly, everyone owns all 24 strengths to varying degrees. The VIA framework encourages individuals to showcase their signature strengths—those that are most energizing and natural to them—and use them intentionally in daily life.

Practical Implications

The VIA Survey, available globally and used in schools, workplaces, and therapeutic settings, helps individuals discover and apply their top strengths. Research has proven the effectiveness of this strength-based approach.

- Increase engagement and satisfaction in work and relationships.
- Build resilience and a sense of purpose.
- Help reach goals by being self-aware and aligned.

A person whose primary strength is curiosity may enjoy discovering new ideas, trying out hobbies, or engaging in projects that combine various fields of interest. Utilizing these strengths yields a life that is more purposeful, powerful, and satisfying.

3. Character.org: Fostering Ethical Values in Communities (Late 20th Century–Present)

Character.org, formerly known as the Character Education Partnership, is a U.S.-based nonprofit organization dedicated to advancing character development in schools, organizations, and communities. It has an essential influence on modern ethical education, not by prescribing fixed traits, but by offering adaptable principles.

The 11 Principles of Effective Character Education

Rather than a strict list of virtues, Character.org promotes flexibility and systemic transformation using its 11 Principles, a framework for embedding character into school culture.

Commonly emphasized ethical values include:

- Respect
- Responsibility

- Trustworthiness
- Fairness
- Caring
- Citizenship

These values promote moral excellence and civic responsibility in both students and institutions.

Practical Implications

Character.org changes the focus from personal self-improvement to building a shared character culture.

- Principle 1 states that schools should promote both academic performance and moral character, creating a balanced environment for learning and ethics.
- Teachers can include fairness in social studies lessons, allowing students to examine justice through historical examples.
- Adults act as role models by demonstrating respect in all their interactions.
- Schools and organizations should incorporate character into their policies, practices, and relationships to ensure that values are practiced, not just taught.

4. Stephen Covey: Principle-Centered Habits (Late 20th Century)

Stephen R. Covey, author of the well-known book The 7 Habits of Highly Effective People, is essential to any discussion about modern character development. Covey's work highlighted that actual effectiveness comes from character, not charisma.

Character Ethic vs. Personality Ethic

According to Covey, a significant portion of 20th-century success literature shifted toward what he termed the Personality Ethic, emphasizing outwardly visible qualities such as charm, image, and social skills. Even though these attributes are essential, they will not lead to long-term success on their own.

He promoted the Character Ethic's resuscitation, highlighting fundamental principles like:

- Integrity
- Humility
- Fidelity
- Temperance
- Courage
- Justice
- Patience
- Industry
- Simplicity
- The Golden Rule states that you should treat people as you would like to be treated.

Covey argues that upholding high moral standards is essential for achieving success in both personal and professional spheres. Without them, even the most talented or endearing person could fail.

The 7 Habits: Reflecting Underlying Character Principles

Stephen Covey's 7 Habits of Highly Effective People are not just tools for productivity; they represent essential character values that promote lasting personal and business growth. Every habit is connected to lasting principles that shape strong leadership and integrity.

1. Be proactive—accept accountability for your actions, exercise initiative, and decide how to react.
2. Start with a clear vision—Keep your goals in mind and base your choices on your principles.
3. Put First Things First—Emphasizes integrity, discipline, and prioritizing what is important over what is just urgent.
4. Thinking win-win means showing respect, being fair, and believing there is enough for everyone to gain something.
5. First, try to understand others before you seek to understand yourself. It needs empathy, humility, and active listening, which are signs of a mature character.
6. Synergize —values diversity, teamwork, and creative collaboration.
7. Sharpen the Saw—This principle encourages ongoing improvement in physical, emotional, mental, and spiritual health.

Practical Implications

Covey highlighted that actual effectiveness starts with universal, internal principles. For instance, "Seek First to Understand" promotes sympathetic listening while exhibiting modesty, restraint, and sincere regard. Like other habits, this one requires a strong character that has been cultivated via life experiences and conscious effort.

5. Character Development: Similarities and Differences

This chapter examines various character development theories, including those found in modern psychology, world religions, self-help books, and ancient philosophy. Despite differences, several shared themes and important distinctions persist.

Shared Connections

- Throughout history and in various cultures, we have consistently held virtues like honesty, fairness, justice, courage, compassion, kindness, responsibility, and respect in high regard. These essential traits offer a straightforward path to living with integrity.
- Habit and Practice: Character is not formed by chance; it is shaped through deliberate and consistent effort.
    - Aristotle taught habituation.
    - Religious traditions emphasize spiritual discipline.
    - Franklin used daily self-tracking.
    - Covey advocated for consistent, principle-based habits.

Together, these models demonstrate that repetition and commitment are crucial to character development.

- Inner-Outer Connection: Most frameworks agree that external behavior comes from internal beliefs, values, and attitudes. Real change starts from the inside, and your actions show that it is happening.
- Mentors and community play an essential role. Religious leaders, role models, and educators all agree that character develops best in supportive environments. Communities that promote accountability, support, and motivation help individuals grow more rapidly.

Significant Divergences

- Sources of Authority:
    - Religious traditions use divine revelation and sacred scripture to shape character.

- Aristotelian and other philosophical systems rely on observation and logical inquiry.
- Evidence-based psychological models like VIA are grounded in scientific research.
- Franklin's approach was realistic and centered on developing oneself by actual experimentation.

Each source influences a character's internalization and knowledge.

- Focus Areas:
  - VIA emphasizes strengths by recognizing and improving what is already working well.
  - Franklin focused on weaknesses, trying to improve personal flaws.
  - Character.org encourages ethical values in group settings.
  - Religious systems usually emphasize virtues and the need to overcome sin, which leads to a moral change based on faith.
- Structure and Scope:
  - Some frameworks provide brief lists, such as the Fruits of the Spirit, Franklin's 13 Virtues, and Covey's 7 Habits.
  - Some topics are wide-ranging and complicated, such as VIA's 24 Strengths or the discussions about sins and virtues in theology.

The extent of detail and organization differs significantly, impacting how easily people can use the model.

- **Universality vs. Specificity:**
  - Systems like VIA or Aristotle's ethics are said to be relevant across different cultures.

- Religious frameworks are strong but usually specific to certain faiths and their beliefs. This can be an advantage in similar communities but a difficulty in diverse or non-religious environments.

Addressing the "Shadow Side"

Most models usually emphasize positive traits. However, few discuss the negative aspects—the possible downsides of overused or misapplied strengths:

- Determination can turn into stubbornness.
- It is easy for confidence to slip into conceit.
- Compassion can lead to burnout if boundaries are not maintained.

A complete character model should also help people in:

- Identifying blind spots
- Handling imbalances or incorrect beliefs
- Viewing common strengths as potential risks

Final Thoughts: Upgrading Your Internal Operating System

This character analysis shows a clear and detailed understanding of building character in today's world. Building a complete system is tough. It must strike a balance between its advantages and disadvantages, be easy to comprehend, and consider different points of view. The knowledge acquired here provides valuable resources for personal development, particularly in today's complex workplace.

A commonality throughout the different frameworks examined—philosophical, spiritual, historical, and scientific—is that a well-thought-out approach is necessary to accomplish a significant "Character Reboot."

Conclusion: Selecting Your Character OS Upgrade

Picture character development as a journey through various islands, each filled with unique treasures:

- Early philosophers established the basics of logic and ethics.
- Spiritual traditions offer vital information about living ethically.
- Enlightenment thinkers offered frameworks for personal discipline and growth.
- Modern psychology provides research-backed frameworks for tangible change.

Each plays a vital role. No single model provides a one-size-fits-all solution, but together, they illustrate the power and complexity of your internal "Character Operating System."

Businesspeople seeking a fresh start often struggle with establishing a clear system. A simple but complete framework is needed—one that:

- It includes a wide range of traits.
- Balances assets and liabilities.
- Provides practical solutions to personal challenges.
- It is organized, clear, and simple to use.

Think of it as an improved file system for a digital device. It should facilitate easy navigation, efficient processing, and seamless integration with your core values and beliefs.

Thomas Edison

"What a man's mind can create, man's character can control."

Welcome to Character OS Reboot.

Thank you for reading my book.

I hope you received a lot of value from it.

Please scan this QR code to receive a 15% discount on the purchase of the Companion Workbook, and to sign up for "Character Cookie," our Monthly Character Newsletter, where we answer the questions submitted by you, the readers, and supporters of Character OS Reboot.

I will also ask you to submit a review of the book using a link. It will help me reach a larger audience.

We will stay in touch if you scan the code and sign up. You can unsubscribe at any time and for any reason.
Discover more at: CharacterOsReboot.com

Whether everyone is watching, or no one is watching, I owe it to myself **to Be, to Feel to Do and to Become** my very best self! Dr. A

BENJAMÍN ALICEA-LUGO, PhD

www.ingramcontent.com/pod-product-compliance
Lightning Source LLC
Chambersburg PA
CBHW052025070526
44584CB00016B/1908